3. Shake paint (and textile medium) thoroughly before using. Pour a small puddle of paint onto your palette. (A plastic plate makes a good palette.) If you are using acrylic paint and textile medium, pour an equal amount of textile medium next to the paint puddle. Mix the textile medium into the paint thoroughly. If you are mixing colors, be sure to mix them thoroughly, too. Have a disposable cup or bowl of water and some paper towels handy to rinse and wipe your brush when necessary.
4. Matching size of brush to the size of the area you wish to paint, dip brush into paint, being careful not to get too much paint on brush. Try not to get paint into the metal part of the paintbrush. Wipe any excess paint onto your palette and begin painting your design. Evenly apply a thin, solid coat of paint to each area. Several thin coats of paint may be required to get adequate coverage. Be sure to allow one color to dry before using another color or adding the next coat. It is a good idea to stop and clean your brush occasionally while painting; however, don't leave your paintbrushes standing in water.
5. If paint splatters on your project, try to gently wash it out with soap and water while the paint is still wet; try not to get the whole item wet. Even if you can't get the spot out, you can cover it with a button, a bow, a lace motif, or a dimensional fabric paint design.
6. Allow design to dry completely before redrawing any lost outlines or detail lines with a permanent felt-tip pen.
7. Some paints require heat-setting if the item will be washed; check manufacturers' instructions on bottles. Heat-setting must be done before adding any dimensional fabric paint to the project. When heat-setting, remove freezer paper and T-shirt form or cardboard covered with plastic wrap and follow manufacturer's instructions to heat-set painted design.
8. Allow paint to dry at least 72 hours before washing. Machine wash project on gentle cycle, following paint and/or glue manufacturer's instructions for water temperature. To launder a garment, turn inside out. Hang project to dry.

Using Dimensional Fabric Paints

1. Turn the bottle upside down and let paint fill the tip to keep paint flowing smoothly.
2. Clean the tip often with a paper towel.
3. If the tip becomes clogged, insert a straight pin into the opening or remove the tip and clean with warm water.
4. If a mistake is made, use a paring knife to gently scrape off paint before it dries. Try to gently wash it out with soap and water while the paint is still wet; try not to get the whole item wet. Or, camouflage the mistake by incorporating it into the design.
5. Keep painted project lying flat at least 24 hours to allow the paint to sufficiently set before handling.

AD

1. T ... glue v
2. V ... area v
3. When dry, shake off excess glitter.

OUR PROJECTS

Many of our projects are painted on fabric items such as garments, tote bags, pillow shams, bibs, and a stocking. We decorated and personalized some of our projects by adding trims such as buttons, rickrack, bows, ribbons, jewel stones, lace trims, lace motifs, glitter, and dimensional fabric paints. We sewed or glued the trims to items and used dimensional fabric paint or glue to adhere jewels.

We painted two designs on purchased canvas boards and custom framed them. We added decorated bows to the corners.

In addition, we created some other slightly more involved projects. The instructions for these projects are presented below. You can duplicate these projects with ease as long as the transfer you choose is of similar size.

Princess Box

1. Cut a piece of fabric 2" larger than height of box and large enough to fit around outside of box.
2. Center and glue fabric to outside of box. Turn upper edge to inside of box; glue. Turn lower edge to bottom of box; glue.
3. Cut a piece of low-loft polyester bonded batting same size as top of box lid. Cut painted fabric 1" larger on all sides than box lid.
4. Hot glue batting to box lid. Center painted fabric on box lid. At 1" intervals, clip fabric to ⅛" from top of lid; hot glue clipped edges to side of lid.
5. Insert a length of ribbon in a length of ruffled lace beading. Hot glue beading around side of lid.
6. Tie a bow from several ribbons; hot glue to lid.

Princess Lamp

1. Paint design on a piece of primed canvas.
2. Fuse paper-backed fusible web to wrong side of painted canvas.
3. Using a pressing cloth, fuse canvas to a piece of lightweight cardboard. Cut out design.
4. Decorate lamp with satin ribbon and a fabric bow.
5. Hot glue canvas cutout to lamp.

Continued on pg. 170.

OUR PRECIOUS PALETTE

Part of the appeal of the Precious Moments™ children is their unique colors. Here we've given you the color palette that we used for our painted projects.

Flesh - 1

Hair - 2 or 3

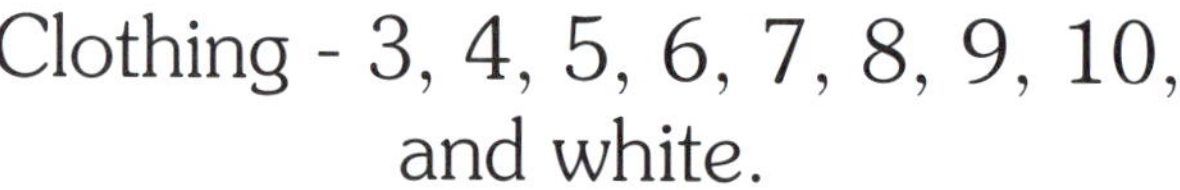

Clothing - 3, 4, 5, 6, 7, 8, 9, 10, and white.

Shoes - 3, 4, 5, 6, 7, 8, 10, 12, and white

Flowers, fish, birds, animals, and other details in your design may be painted any of the colors.

Happy Birdie
What The World Needs
Is Love

Isn't He Precious

The Greatest Of These
Is Love

God Bless our Home
We Gather Together To Ask The Lord's Blessing
I Believe In
The Old Rugged Cross

GUM BALLS
Jest one Penny

Oh What fun It Is To Ride

I'll Give Him My Heart

God's Promises Are Sure

We All Have Our
Bad Hair Days

Toys
Baby Sitting Guide
Games

Jesus Loves Me
Part Of Me
Wants To Be Good

O Come Let Us Adore Him
MOLLY
May All Your Christmases
Be White
Bundles Of Joy
Come Let Us Adore Him

Test Transfer

Not intended for resale.

© 1996, PMI

Bundle Of Joy

Bundle Of Joy

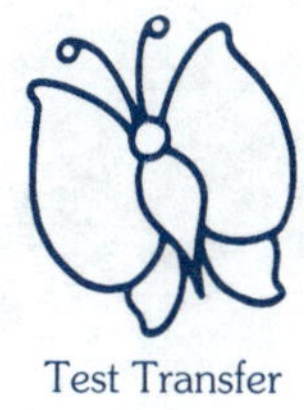

Test Transfer

Jesus Loves Me

Not intended for resale.

© 1996, PMI

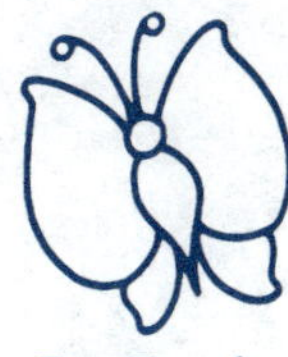

Test Transfer

© 1996, PMI

Not intended for resale.

Baby's First Trip

Test Transfer

Not intended for resale.

© 1996, PMI

Baby's First Trip

Baby's First Trip

Test Transfer

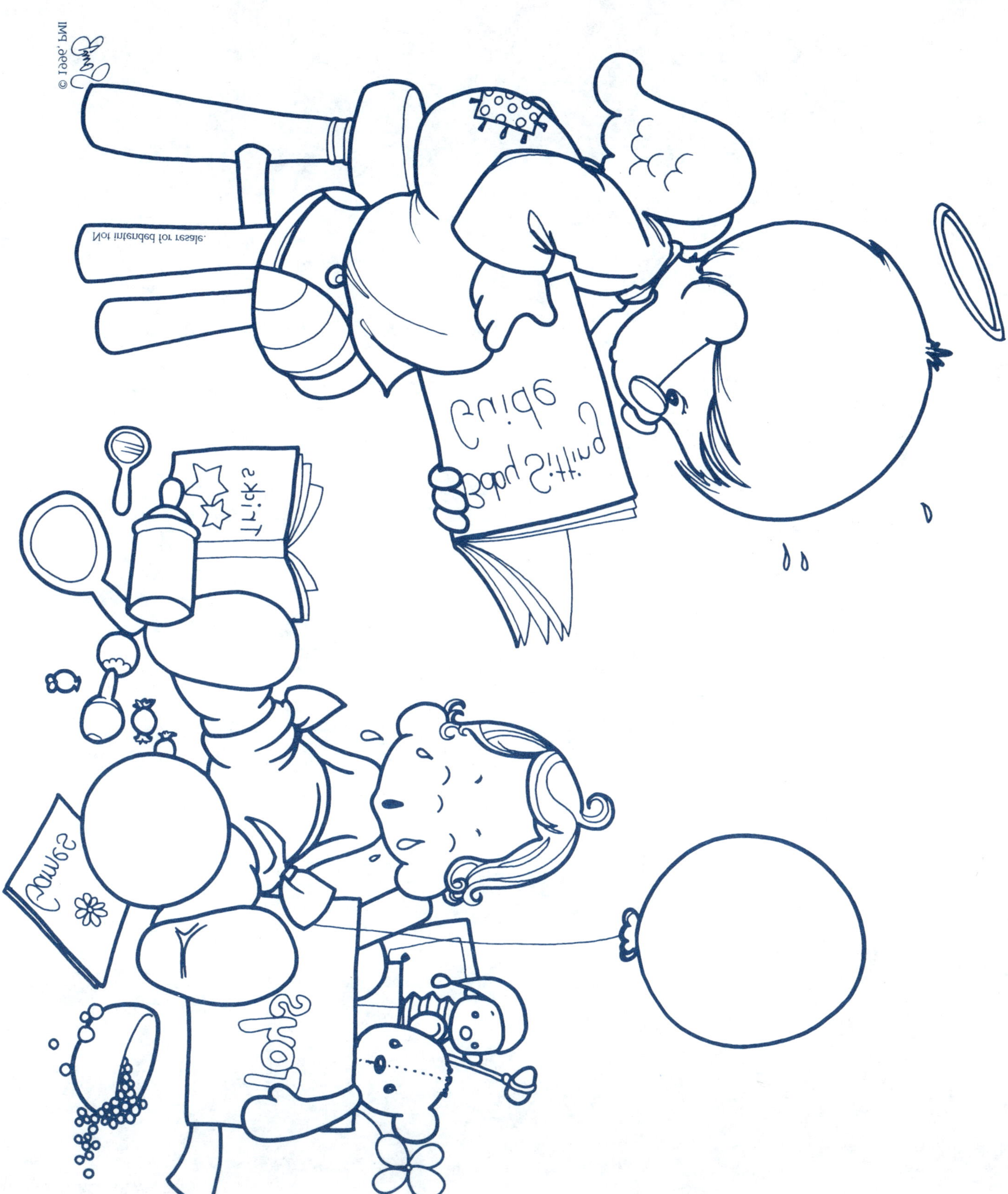

© 1996, PMI
Not intended for resale.

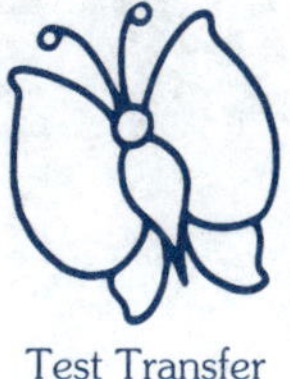

Test Transfer

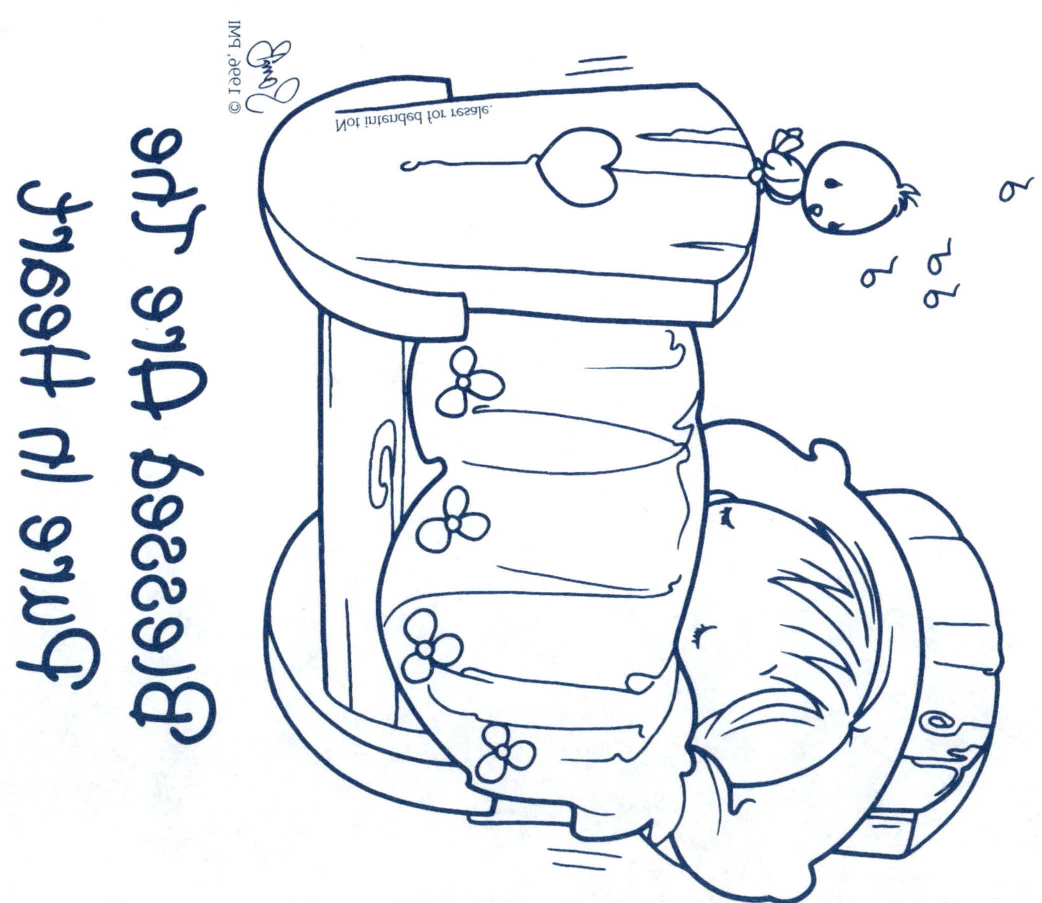

Precious Keepsakes

Blessed Are The Pure In Heart

Blessed Are
Pure In
Precious

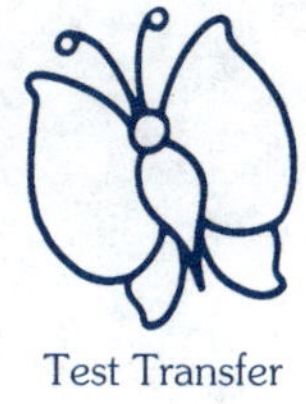

Test Transfer

Part Of Me Wants To Be Good

Part Of Me
Wants To Be Good

Baby Shower

Test Transfer

Baby Shower

© 1996, PMI

Not intended for resale.

Baby Shower

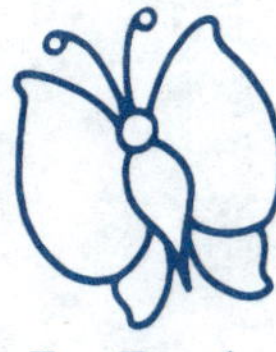

Test Transfer

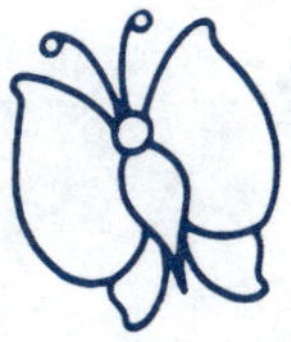

Test Transfer

To Some Bunny Special

© 1996, PMI

Not intended for resale.

To Some Bunny Special

Happy Birdie

Happy Birthd
to Some Bun

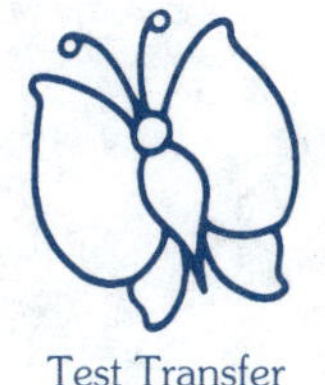

Test Transfer

It's The Birthday Of A King

It's The Birthday Of A King

It's The Birthday
Of A King

Test Transfer
Not intended for resale.
© 1996, PMI

Test Transfer

Not intended for resale.
© 1996, PMI

Test Transfer

Test Transfer

© 1996, PMI

Not intended for resale.

Thinking Of You Is What I Really Like To Do

Thinking Of You Is What I Really Like To Do

Thinking Of You Is What

Test Transfer

© 1996, PMI

Not intended for resale.

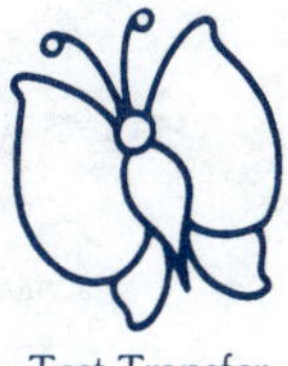

Test Transfer

© 1996, PMI

Not intended for resale.

Test Transfer

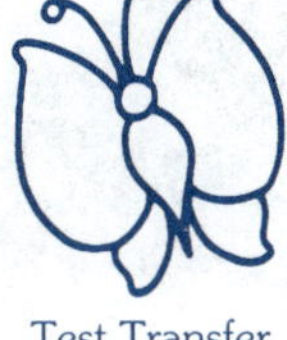

Test Transfer

Test Transfer
Not intended for resale.
© 1996, PMI

Test Transfer
© 1996, PMI
Not intended for resale.

Test Transfer

Bring The Little Ones To Jesus

Bring The Little Ones To Jesus

Test Transfer

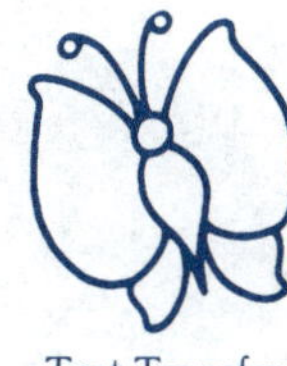

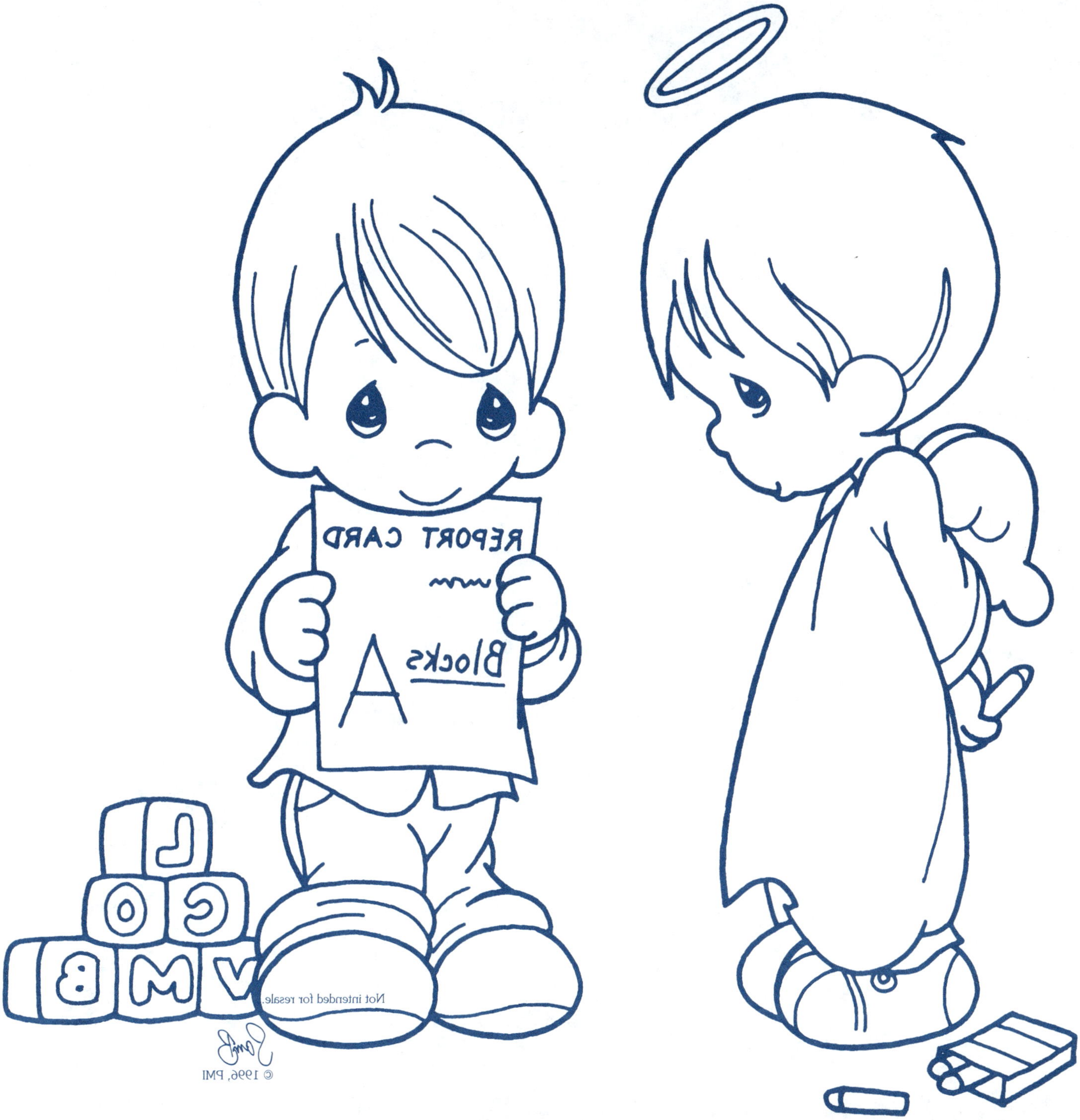
REPORT CARD
Blocks
A
L
G O
B M V
Not intended for resale.
© 1996, PMI

Test Transfer

© 1996, PMI

Not intended for resale.

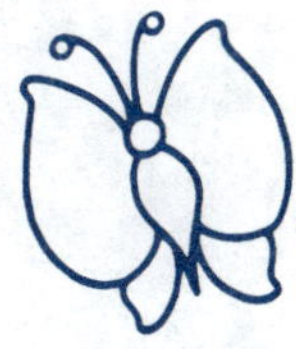

Test Transfer

Not intended for resale.
© 1996, PMI

Test Transfer

© 1996, PMI
Not intended for resale.

Test Transfer

Test Transfer

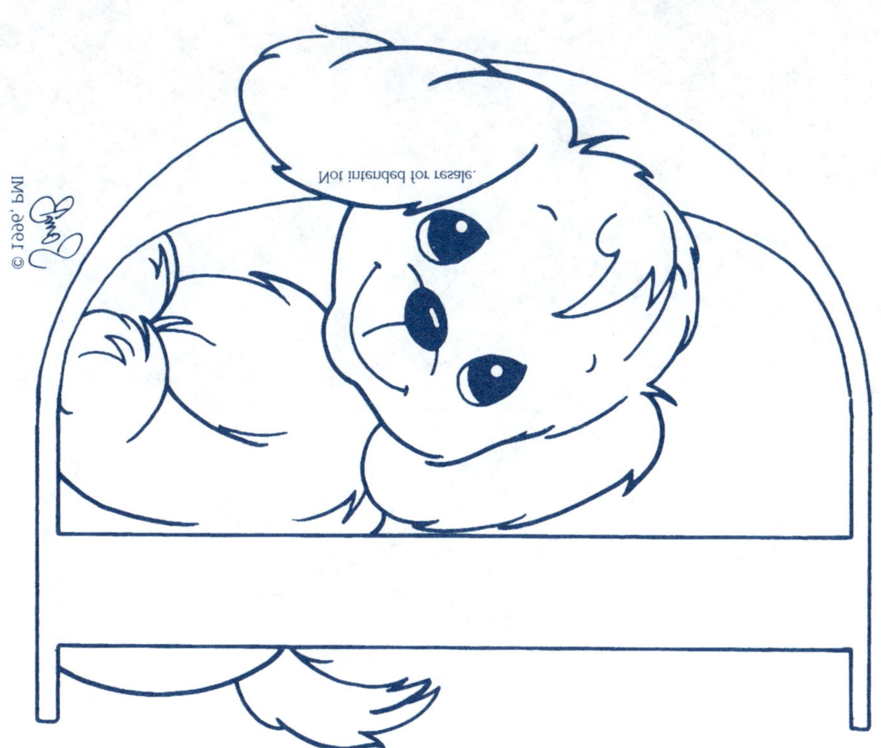

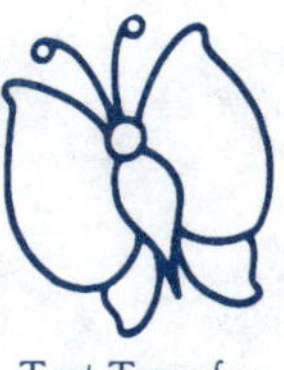
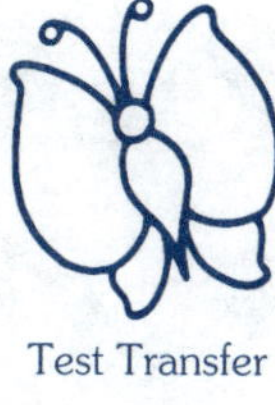

Test Transfer

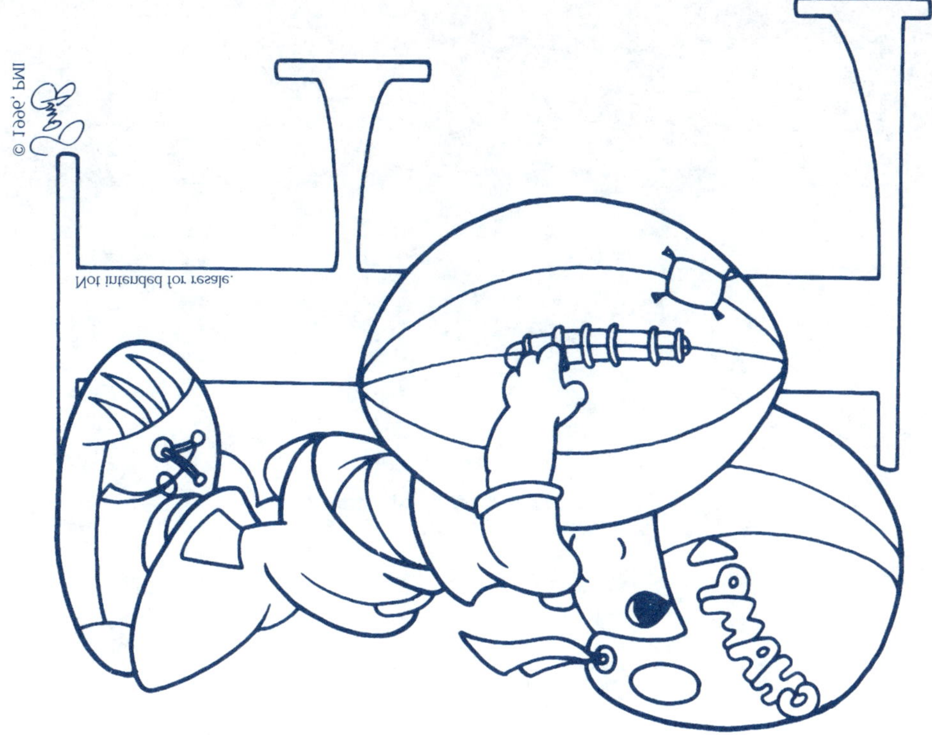

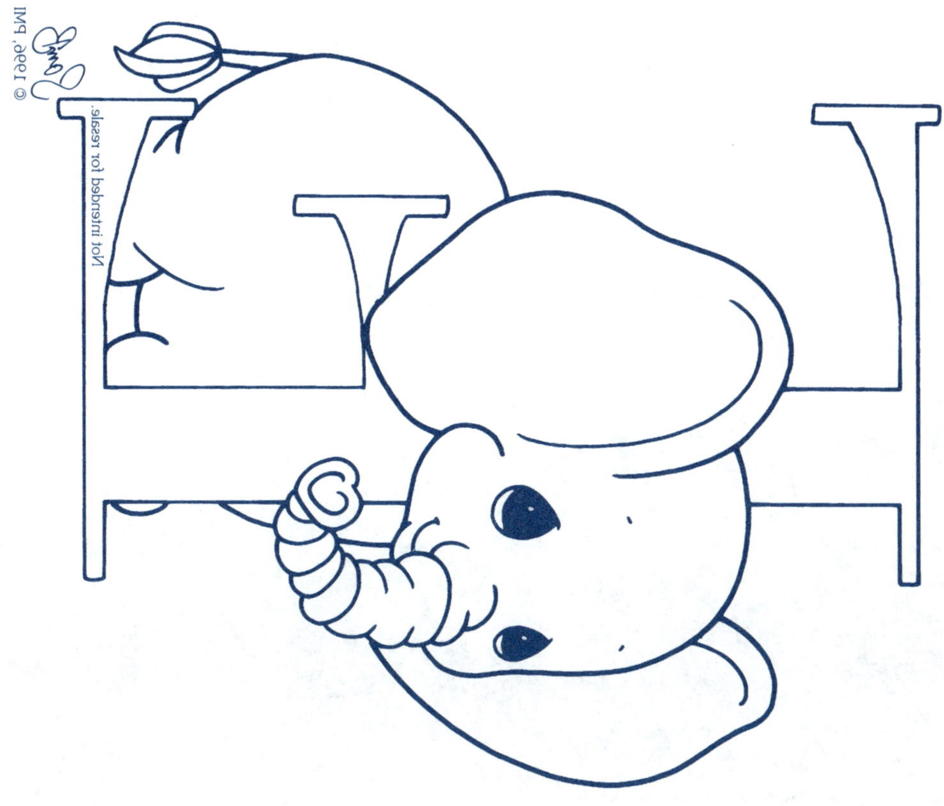

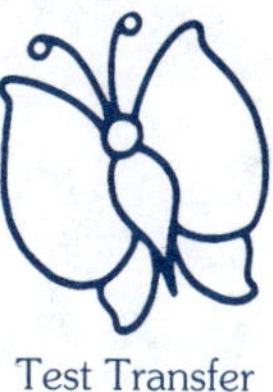

Test Transfer

Test Transfer

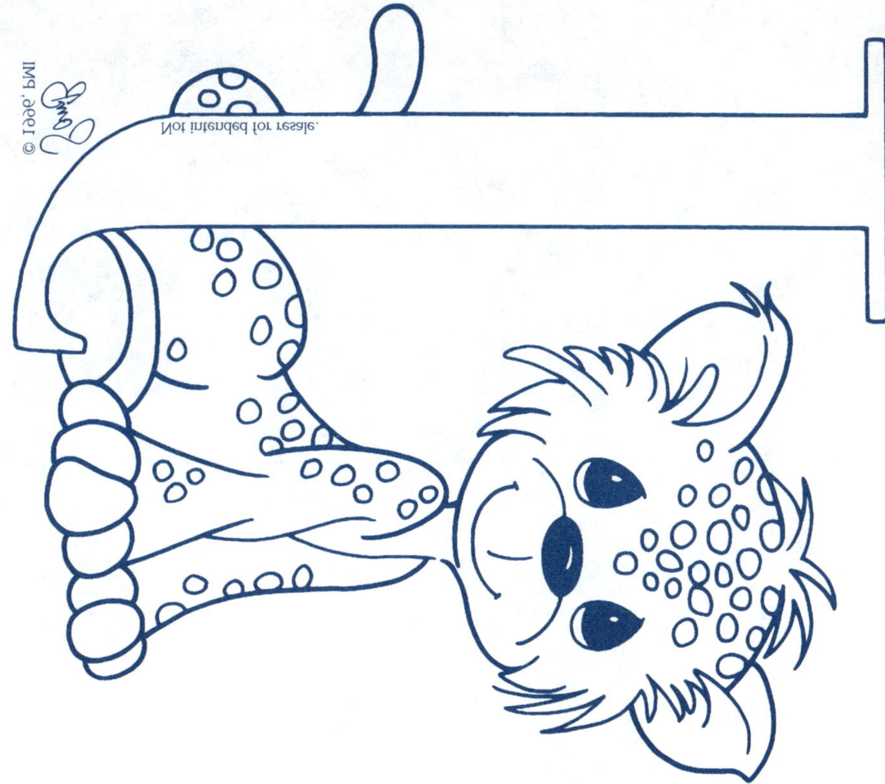

Test Transfer

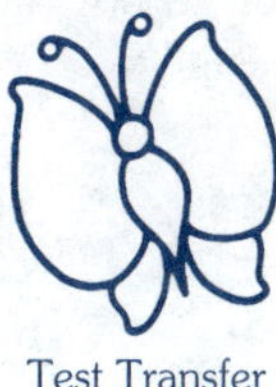

Test Transfer

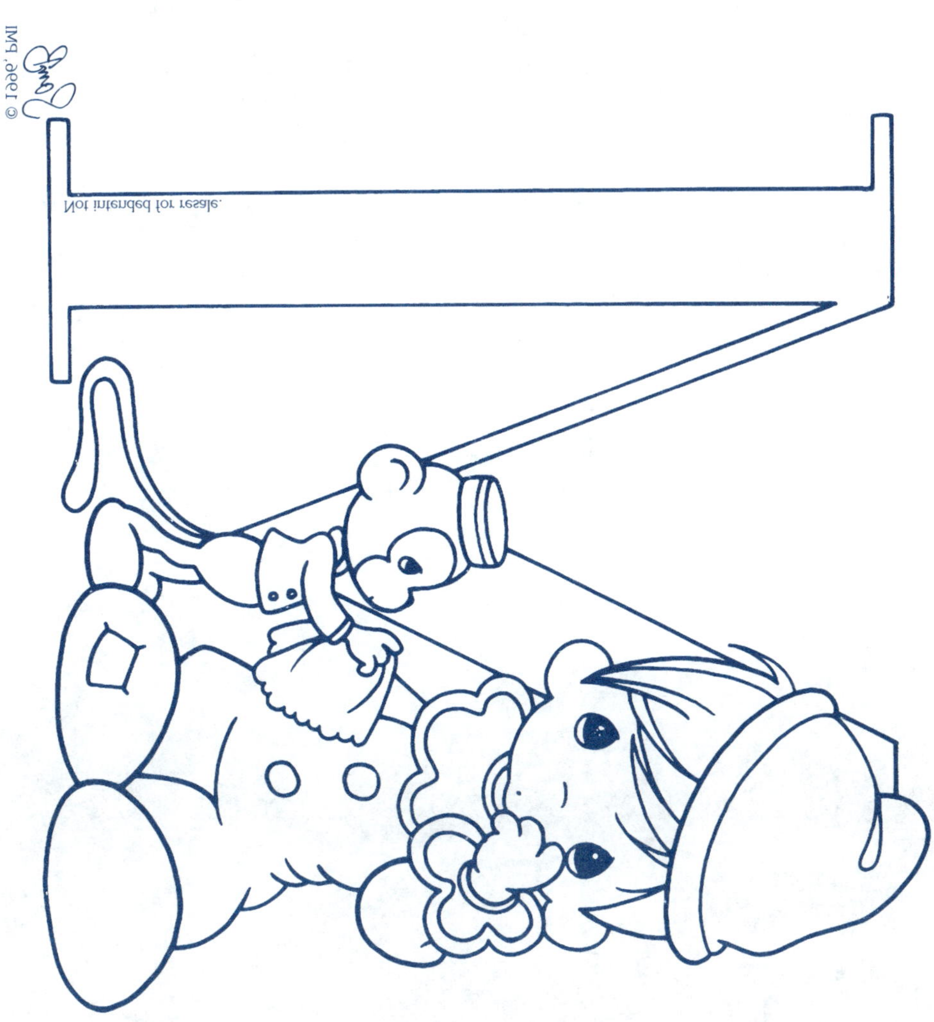

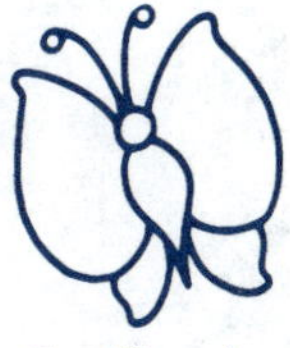

Test Transfer

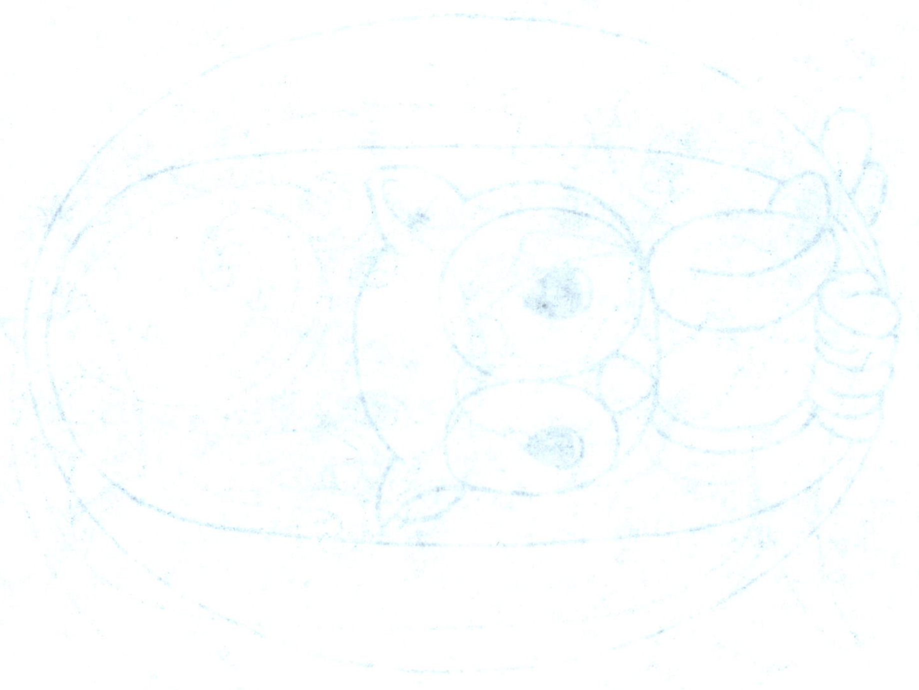

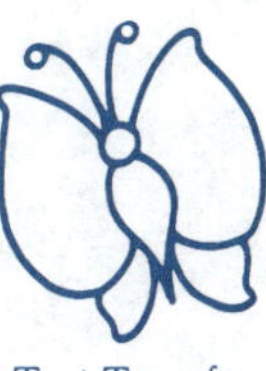

Test Transfer

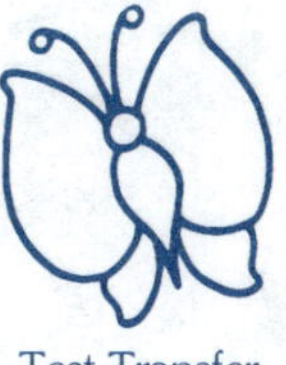

Test Transfer

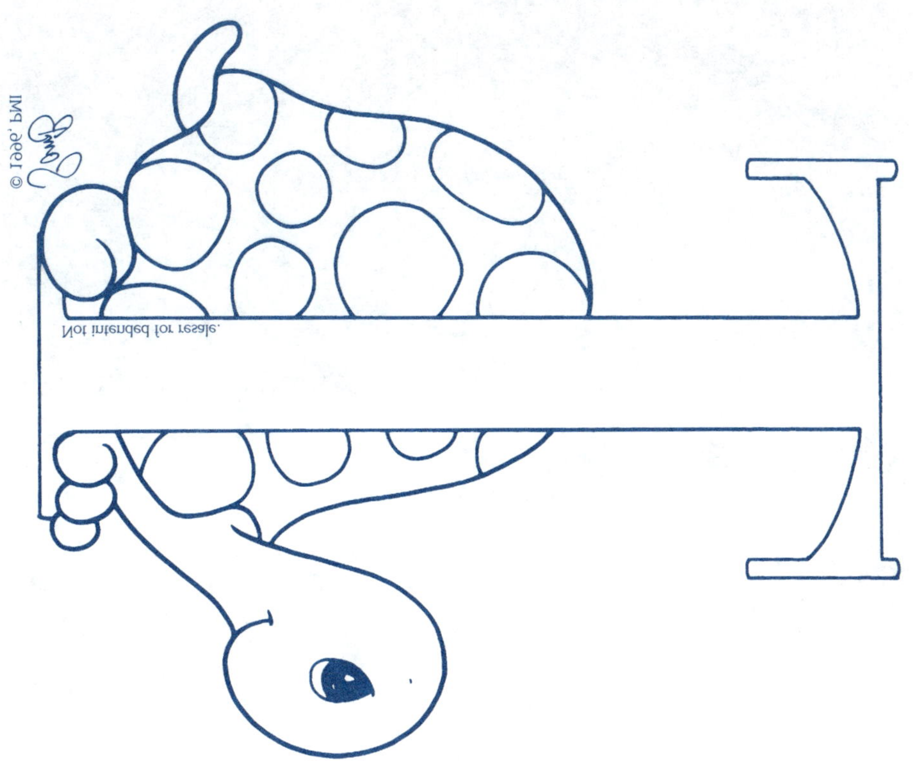

Test Transfer

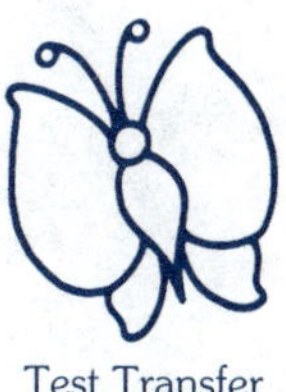

Test Transfer

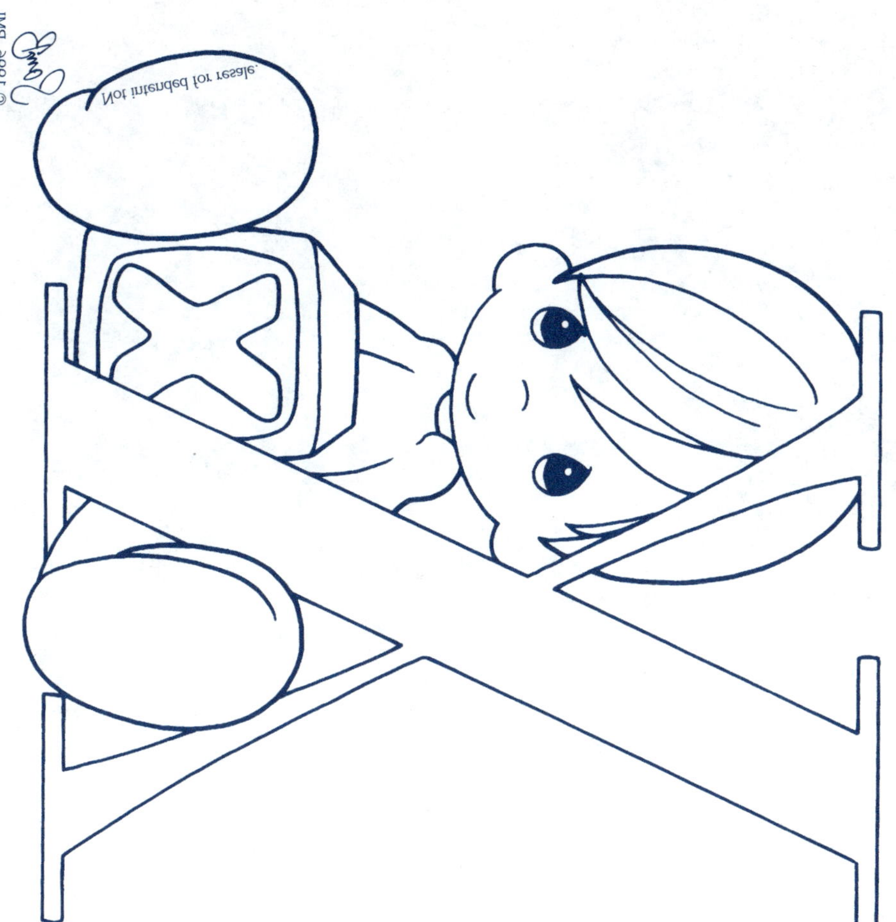

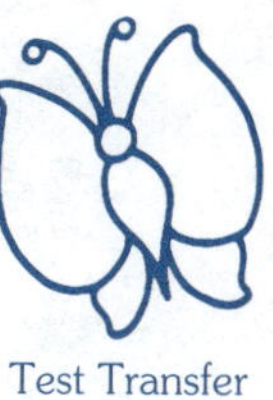

Test Transfer

Test Transfer

Not intended for resale.
© 1996, PMI

Love One Another

Love One Another

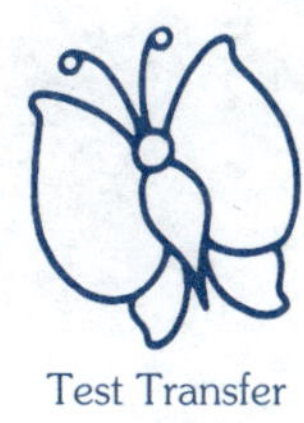

Test Transfer

He
Loves
Me...
He
Loves
Me...

Not intended for resale.

© 1996, PMI

Test Transfer

Love Covers All

Not intended for resale. © 1996, PMI

Love Covers All

Not intended for resale. © 1996, PMI

Love Never Leaves A Mother's Arms

Test Transfer

© 1996, PMI

Not intended for resale.

A Universal Love

A Universal Love

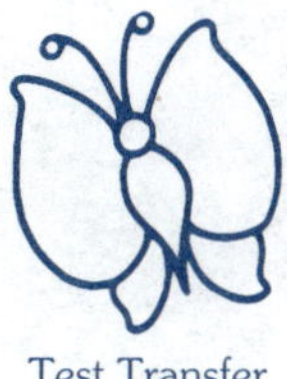

Test Transfer

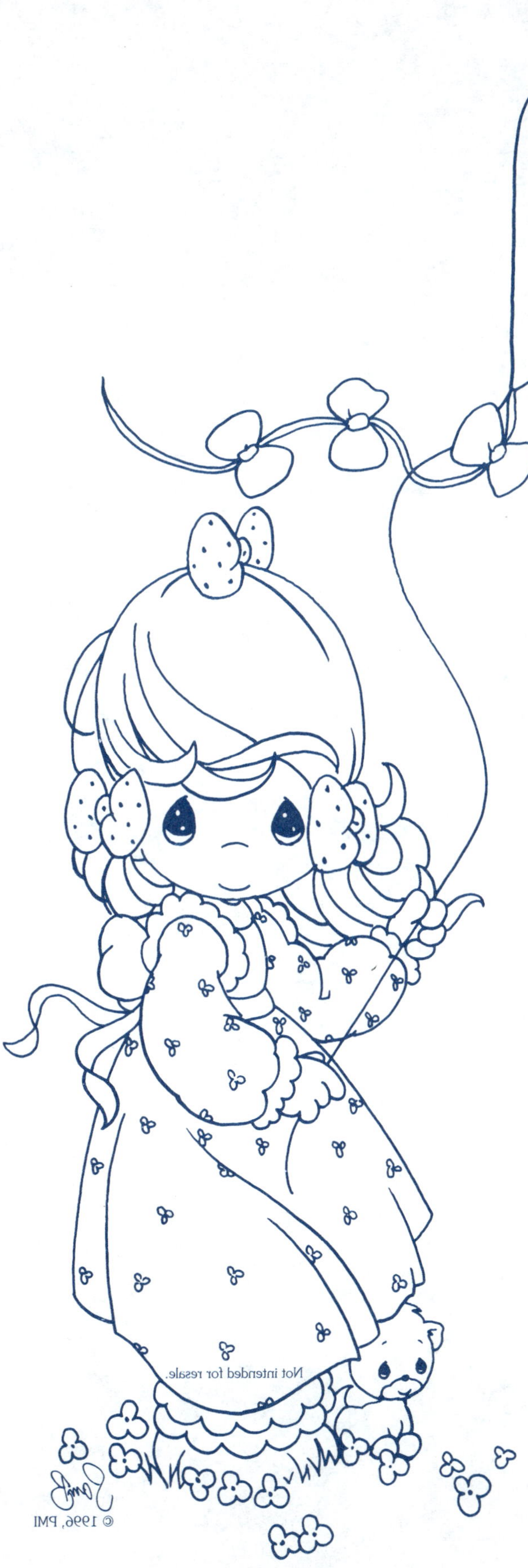

Not intended for resale.
© 1996, PMI

Sending
My
Love
Your
Way

Sending My Love Your Way

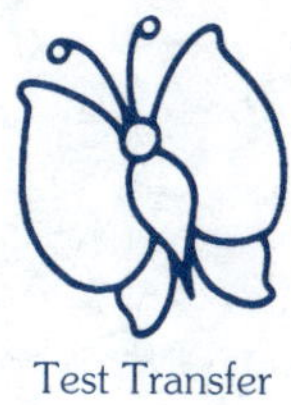

Test Transfer

Our Love Nose No Boundaries

© 1996, PMI

Not intended for resale.

Our Love Nose No Boundaries

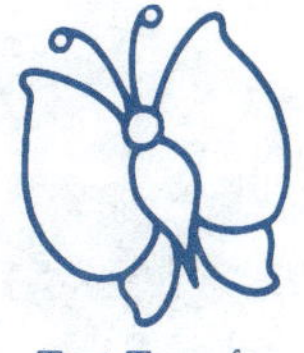

Test Transfer

© 1996, PMI

Not intended for resale.

Love Is Forgiving

Love Is Forgiving

Test Transfer

Not intended for resale.

© 1996, PMI

Our Friendship Is Tied With Love

Our Friendship Is Tied With Love

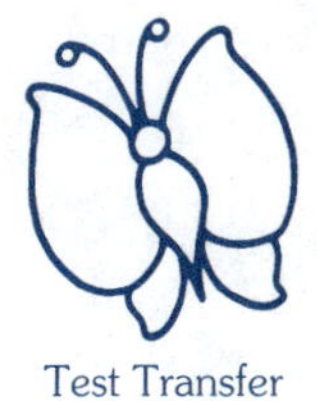

Test Transfer

Not intended for resale.
© 1996, PMI

Sending You Oceans Of Love

Sending You Oceans Of Love

Sending You Oceans Of Love

Like I Do

Test Transfer

Not intended for resale.

© 1996, PMI

Snowbunny Loves You Like I Do

Snowbunny Loves You Like I Do

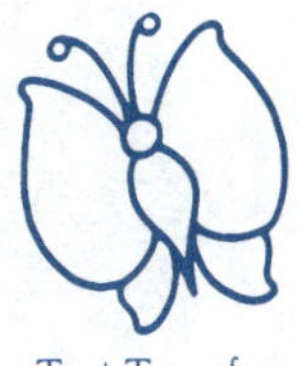

Test Transfer

Not intended for resale.

© 1996, PMI

Love Is Sharing

Love Is Sharing

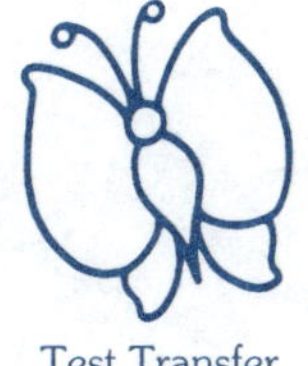

Test Transfer

My Love Will
Never Let You Go

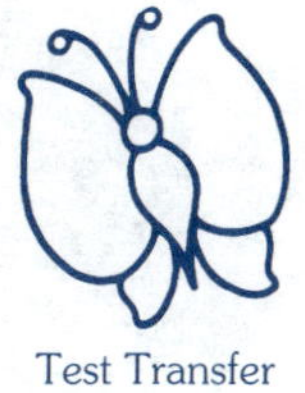

Test Transfer

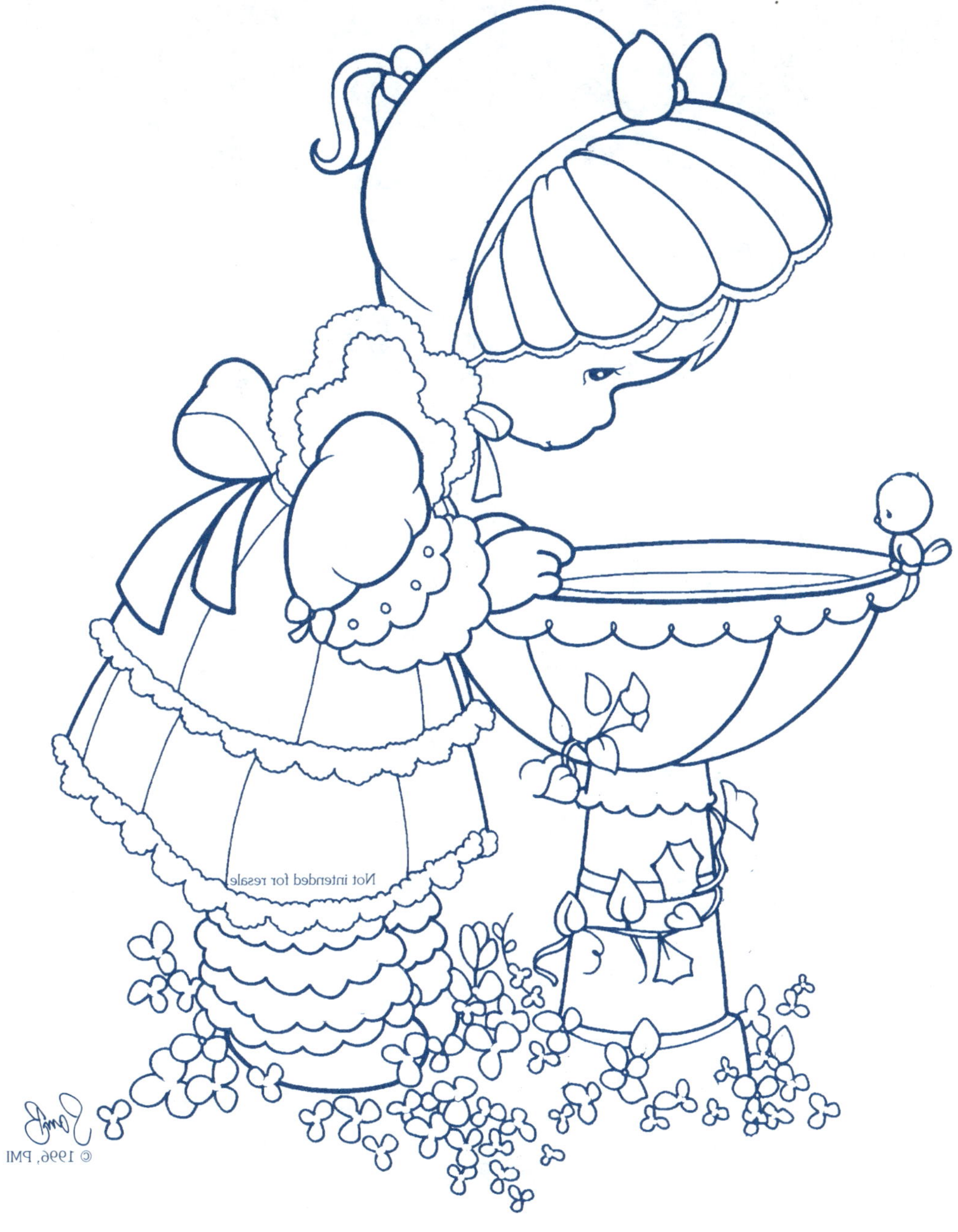

Not intended for resale
© 1996, PMI

A Reflection Of His Love

A Reflection Of His Love

A Reflection Of His Love

Love One Another

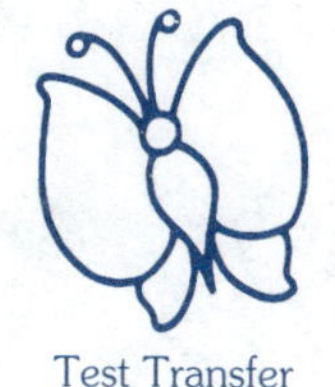

Test Transfer

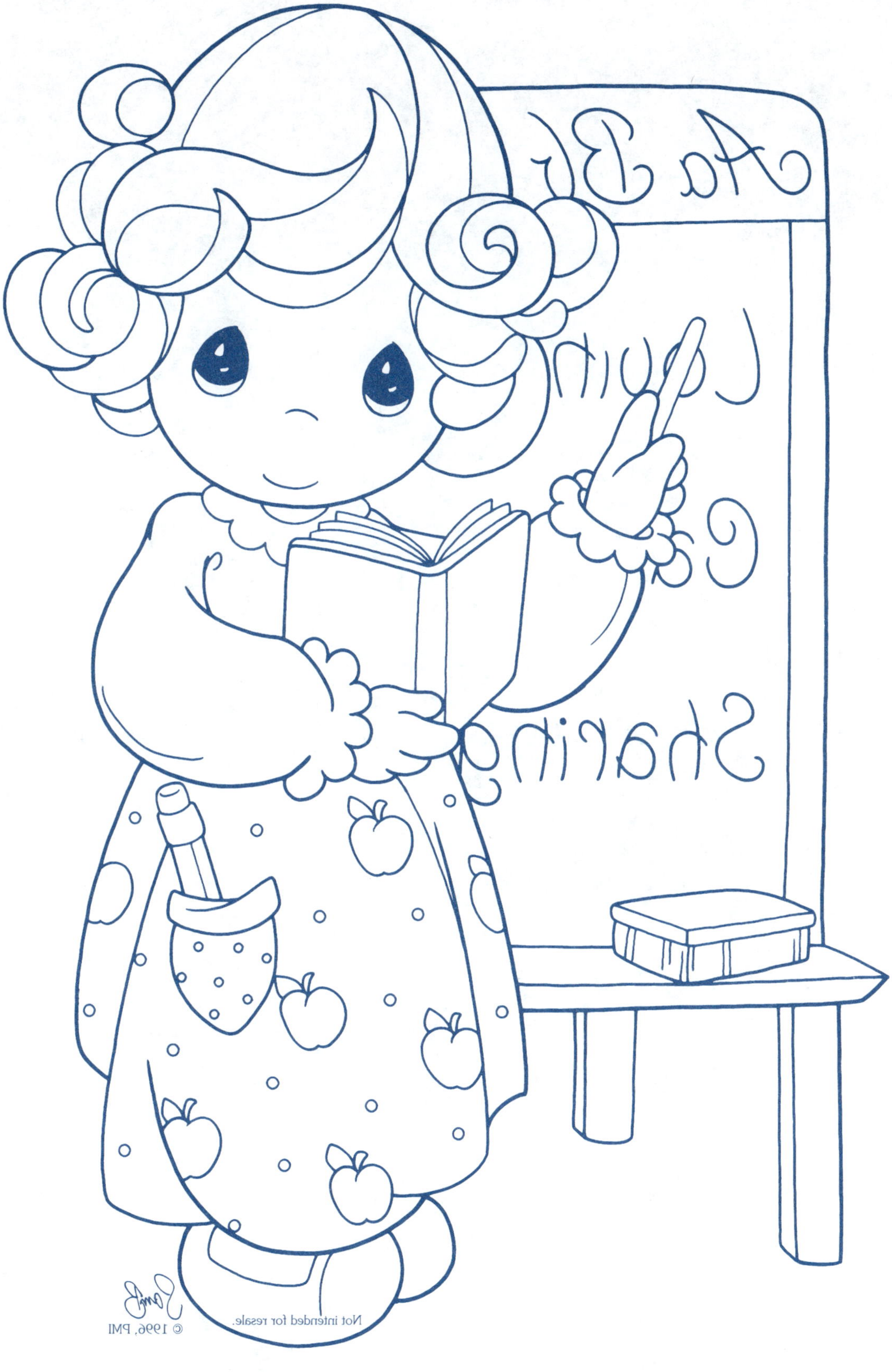

Aa Bb
Loving
Caring
Sharing
Not intended for resale.
© 1996, PMI

Teach Us To Love One Another

Teach Us To Love One Another

Test Transfer

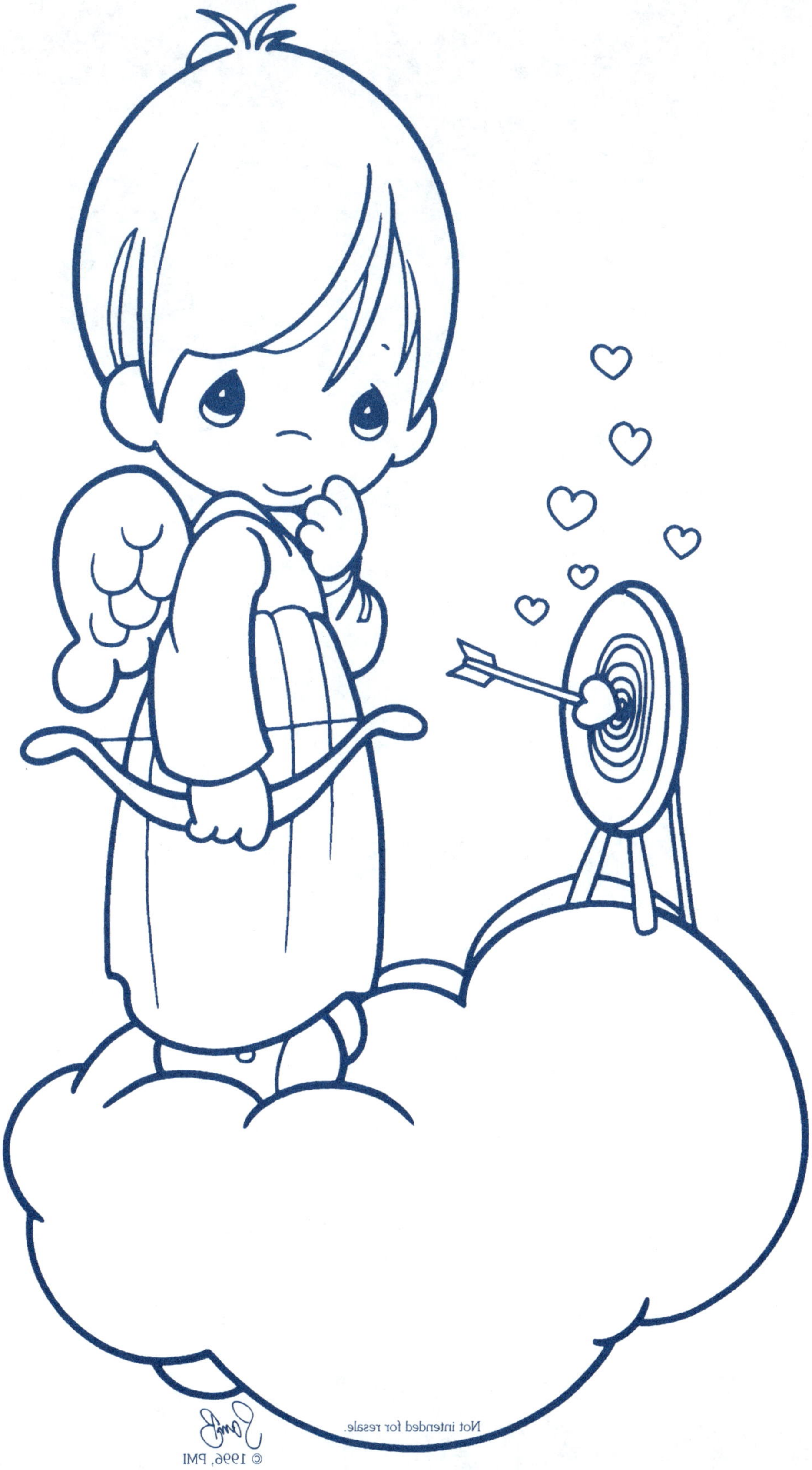

Not intended for resale.

© 1996, PMI

Sending My Love

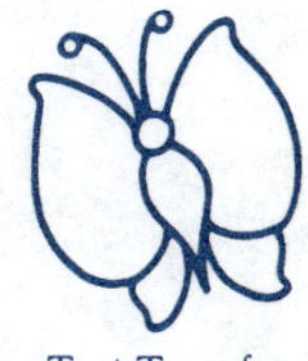

Test Transfer

God Sends The Gift Of Love

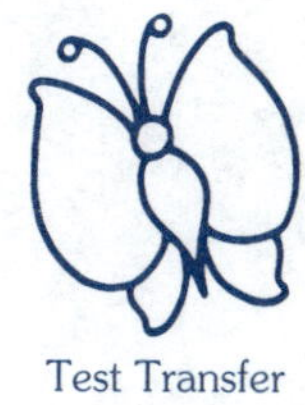

Test Transfer

You Are
The Gift
Of God's
Love

Not intended for resale.

© 1996, PMI

You Are The Gift Of God's Love

You Are
The Gift
Of God's
Love

Test Transfer

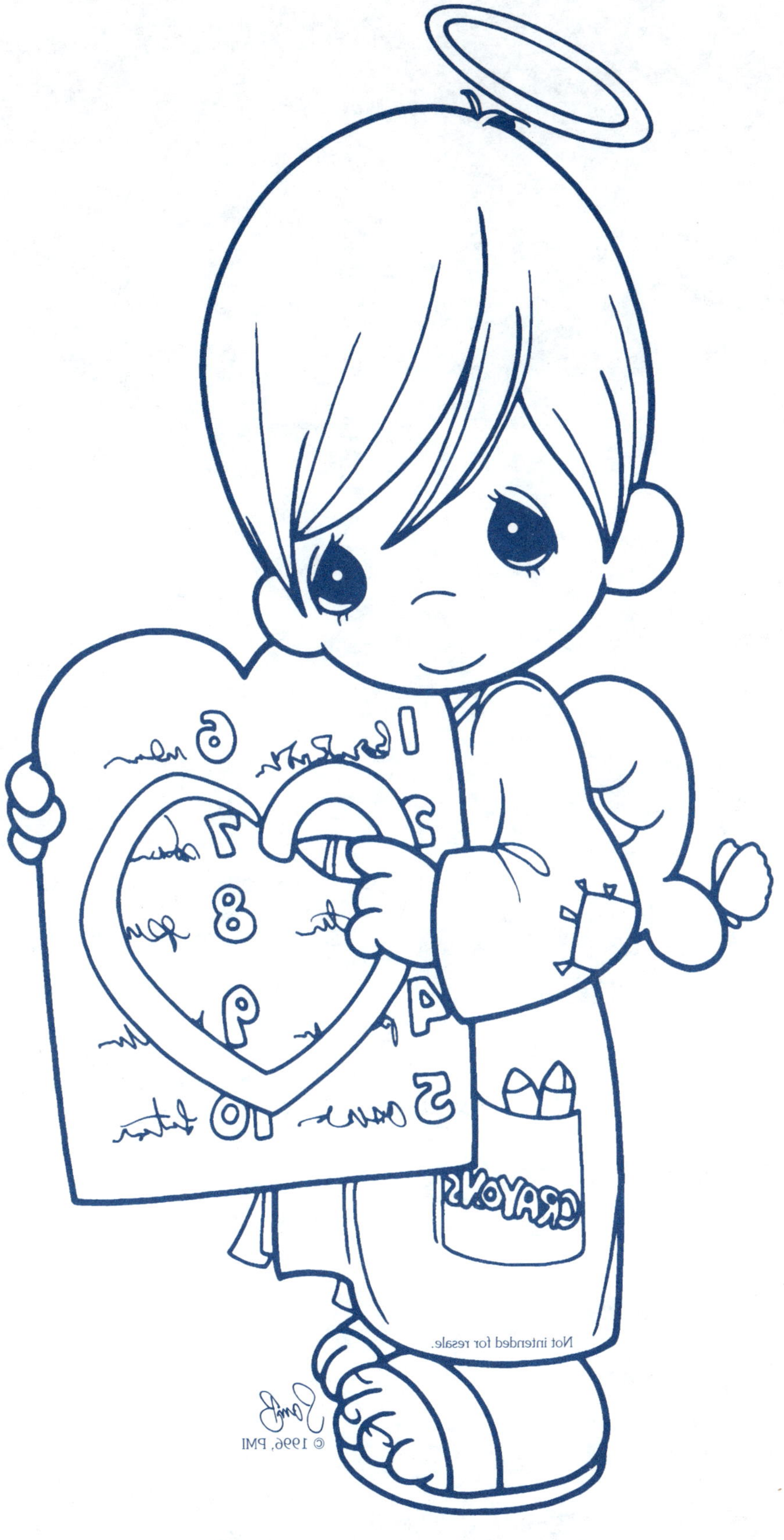

Not intended for resale.

© 1996, PMI

The Greatest Of These Is Love

The Greatest Of These Is Love

The Greatest Of These

Your Love Is So Uplifting

Our Love Is So Uplifting

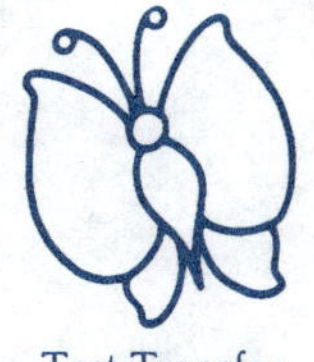

Test Transfer

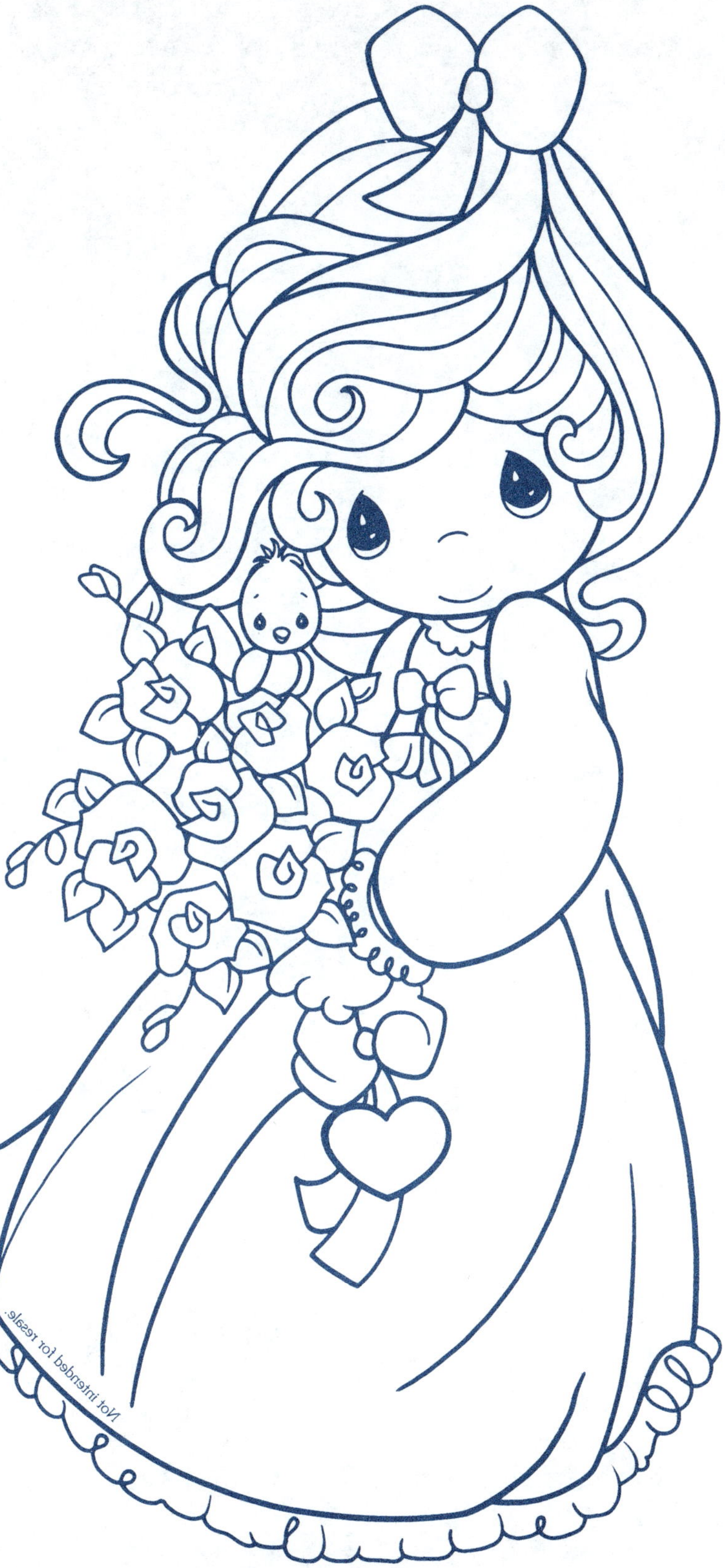

© 1996, PMI
Not intended for resale.

You Are My Happiness

You Are My Happiness

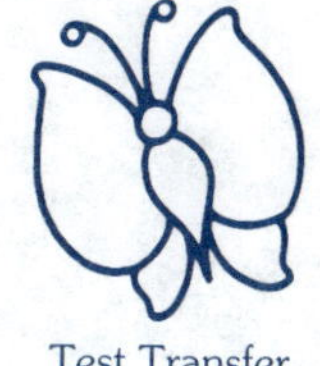

Test Transfer

Not intended for resale.
© 1996, PMI

I'll Always Be Thinking Of You

I'll Always Be Thinking Of You

Test Transfer

Rejoicing With You

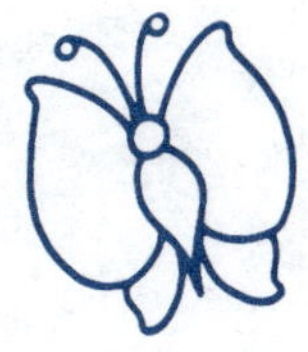

Test Transfer

No. 1

Not intended for resale.

© 1996, PMI

You Are My Once In A Lifetime

You Are My Once

Test Transfer

God Bless Our Years Together

God Bless Our Years Together

God Bless Our Years Together

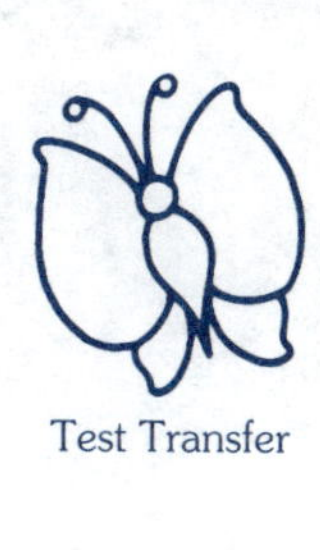

Test Transfer

Not intended for resale.

© 1996, PMI

Test Transfer

You Are An Angel To Me

You Are An Angel To Me

You Are An Angel To Me

Test Transfer

Test Transfer

Not intended for resale.
© 1996, PMI

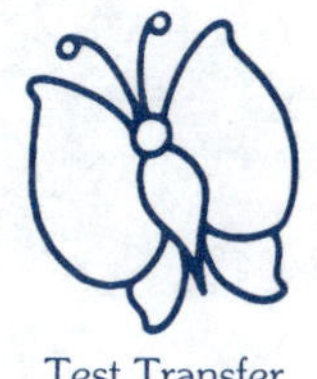

Test Transfer

You're Such A Purr-fect Friend

You're Such A Purr-fect Friend

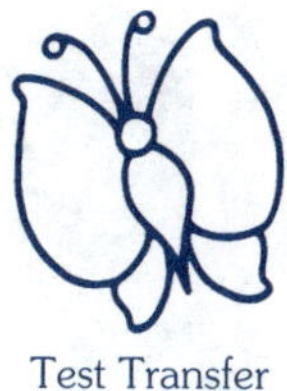

Test Transfer

Our Friendship Is Soda-licious

Your Love Is So Uplifting

Test Transfer

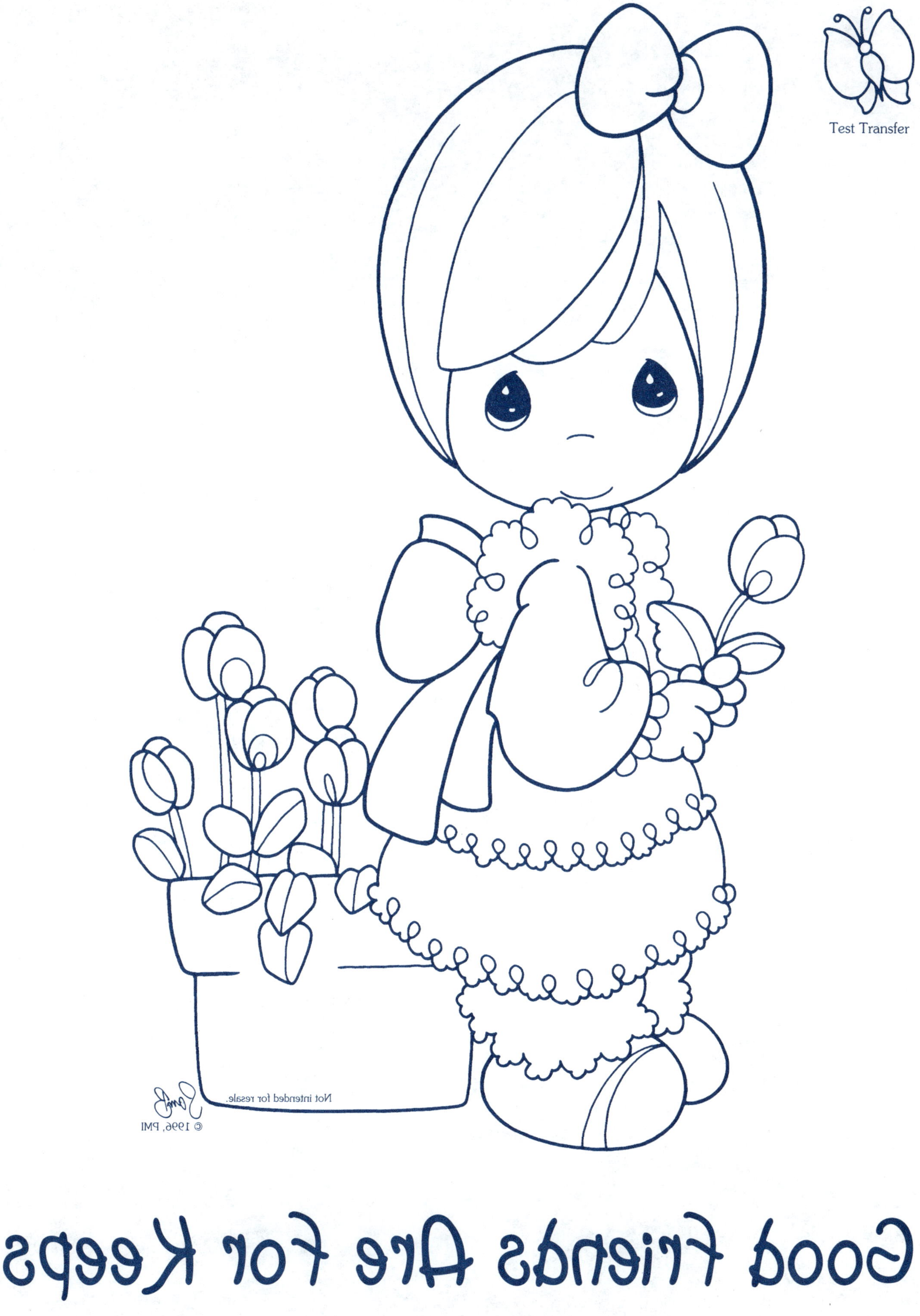

Not intended for resale.

© 1996, PMI

Good Friends Are For Keeps

Good Friends Are For Keeps

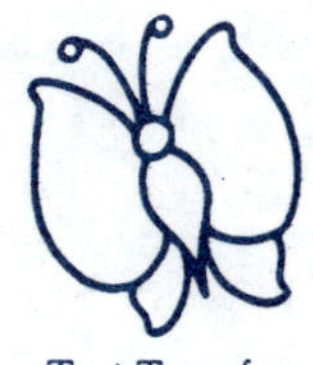

Test Transfer

Make A Joyful Noise

What A Difference You've Made In My Life

Make A Joyful Noise

What A Difference You've Made In My Life

Test Transfer

Not intended for resale.
© 1996, PMI

I'm Hoppy When I'm With You

I'm Hoppy When I'm With You

I'm Happy When I'm With You.

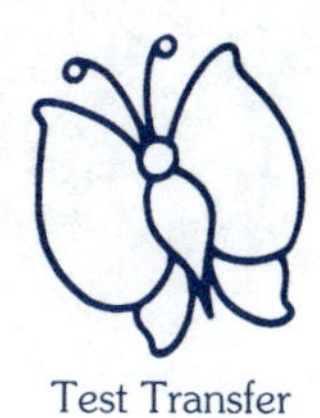

Test Transfer

You've Made A Big Difference In My Life

Not intended for resale.
© 1996, PMI

You've Made A Big Difference In My Life

You've Made A Big Difference In My Life

Test Transfer

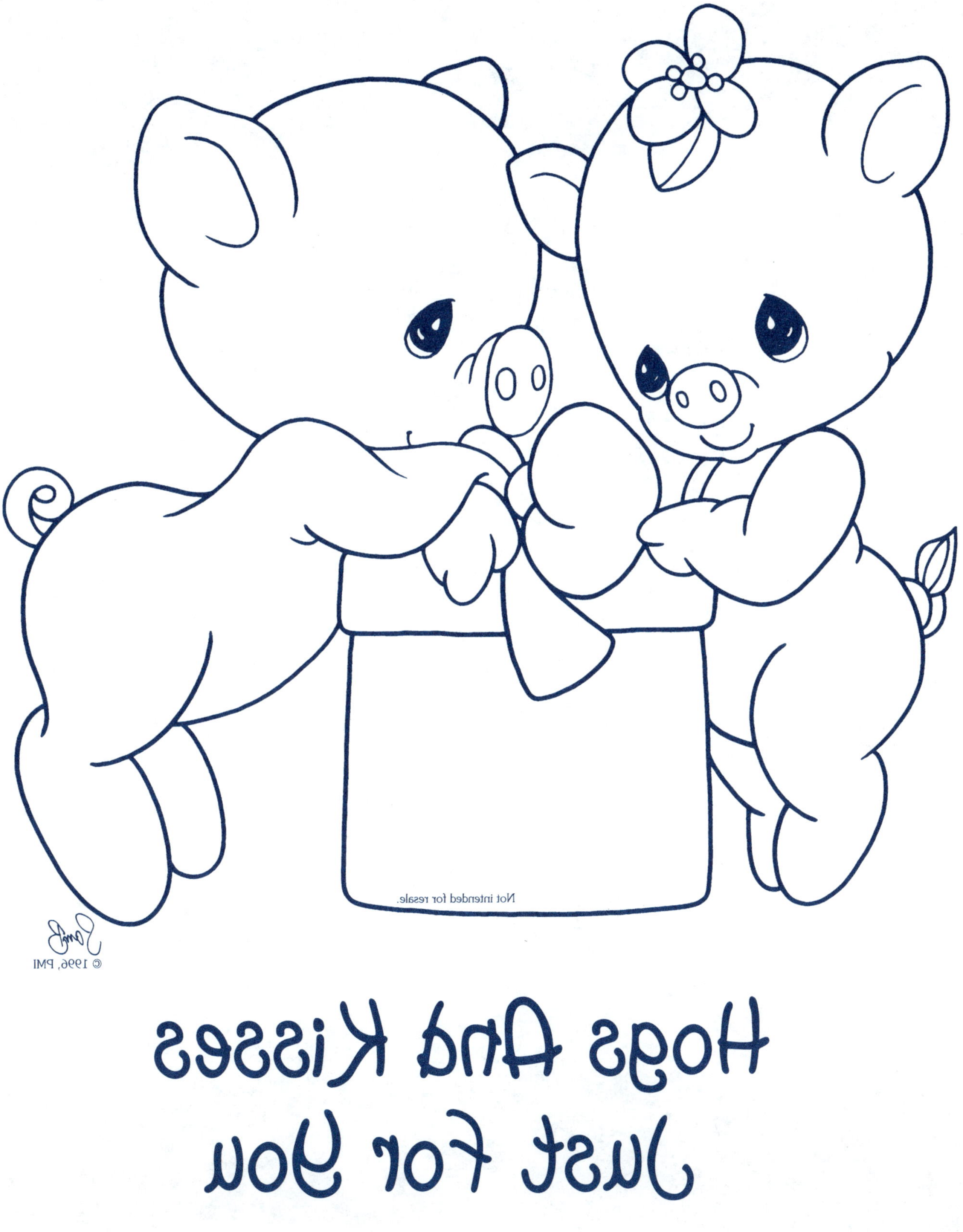

Not intended for resale.

© 1996, PMI

Hogs And Kisses Just For You

Hogs And Kisses
Just for You

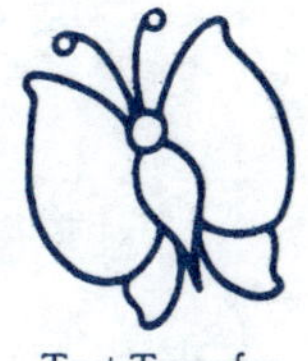

Test Transfer

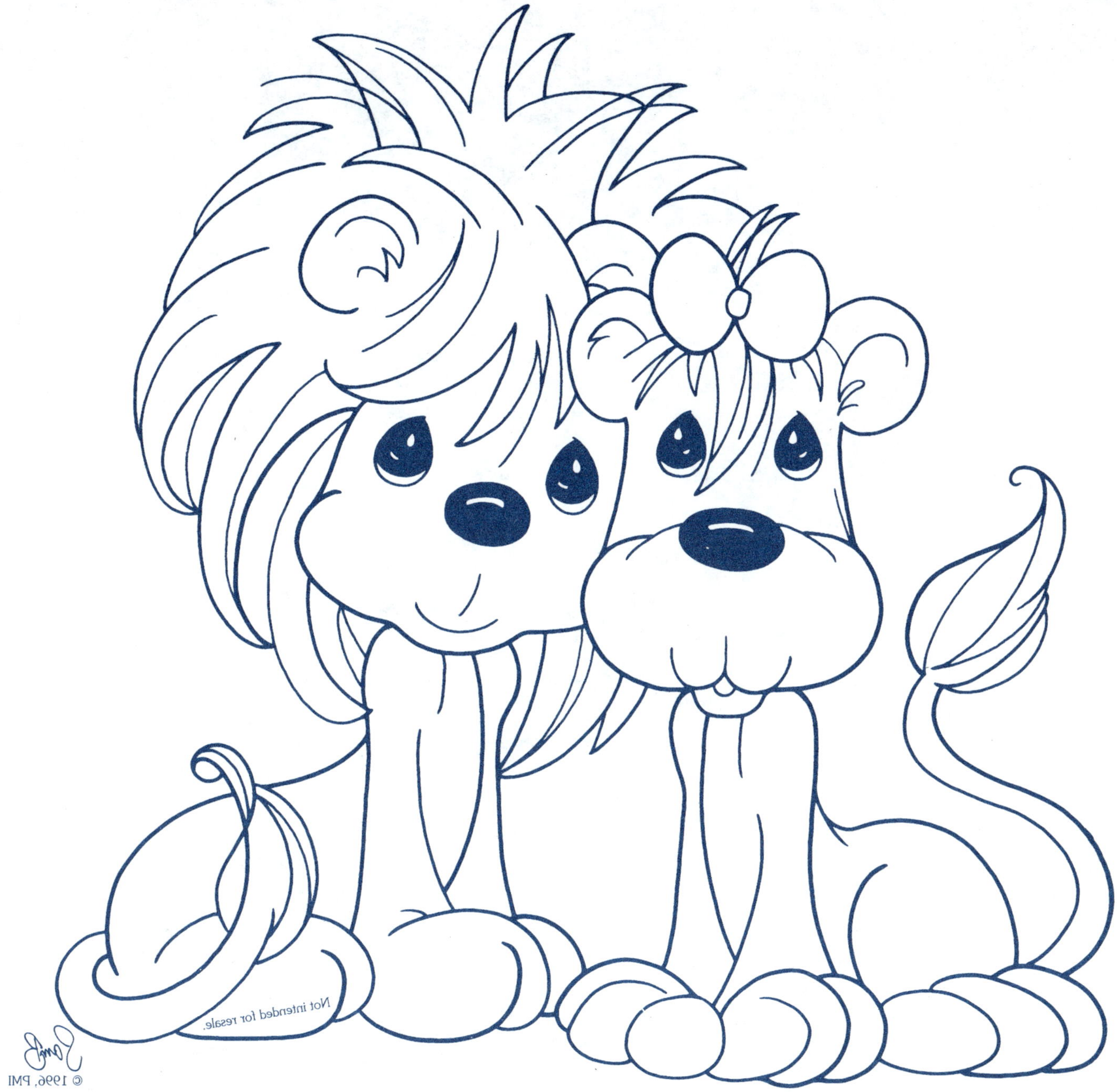

Not intended for resale.
© 1996, PMI

Together We're A Roarin' Success

Together We're A Roarin' Success

Test Transfer

I'd Goat Anywhere With You

Not intended for resale.

© 1996, PMI

I'd Goat Anywhere With You

Joy Is The Music Of Angels

Joy Is The Music Of Angels

Joy Is The Music Of Angels

Love

Test Transfer

© 1996, PMI

Not intended for resale.

Love

Love

Love

Test Transfer

Not intended for resale.

© 1996, PMI

Hope

Hope

Hope

Test Transfer

faith

Not intended for resale.
© 1996, PMI

Faith

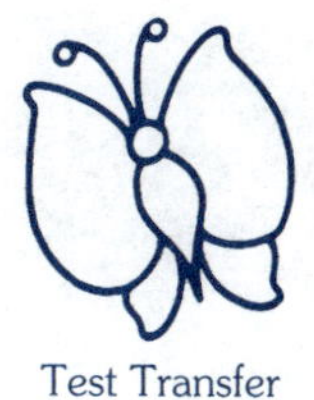

Test Transfer

PAINT

Not intended for resale.

© 1996, PMI

What A Wonderful World

What A Wonderful World

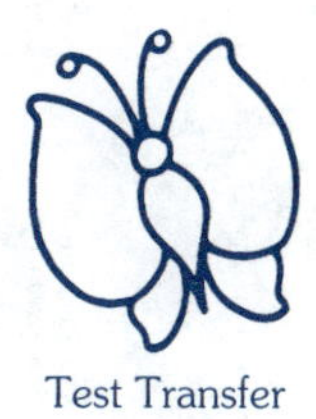

Test Transfer

Love

Not intended for resale.

© 1996, PMI

What The World Needs Is Love

What The World Needs
is Love

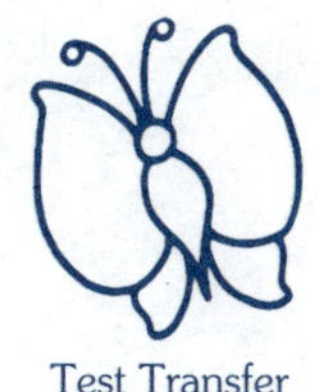

Test Transfer

He
Covers
The
World
With His
Beauty

Not intended for resale.

© 1996, PMI

He Covers The World With His Beauty

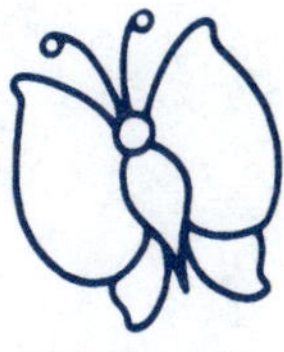

Test Transfer

Loving

Loving

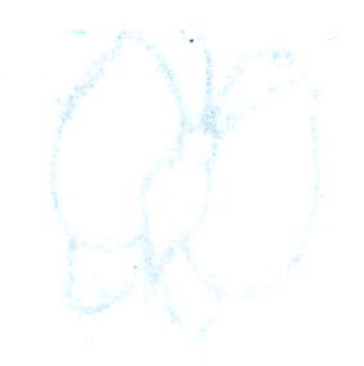

Loving

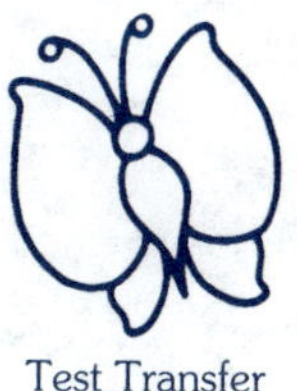

Test Transfer

Not intended for resale.
© 1996, PMI
Caring

Caring

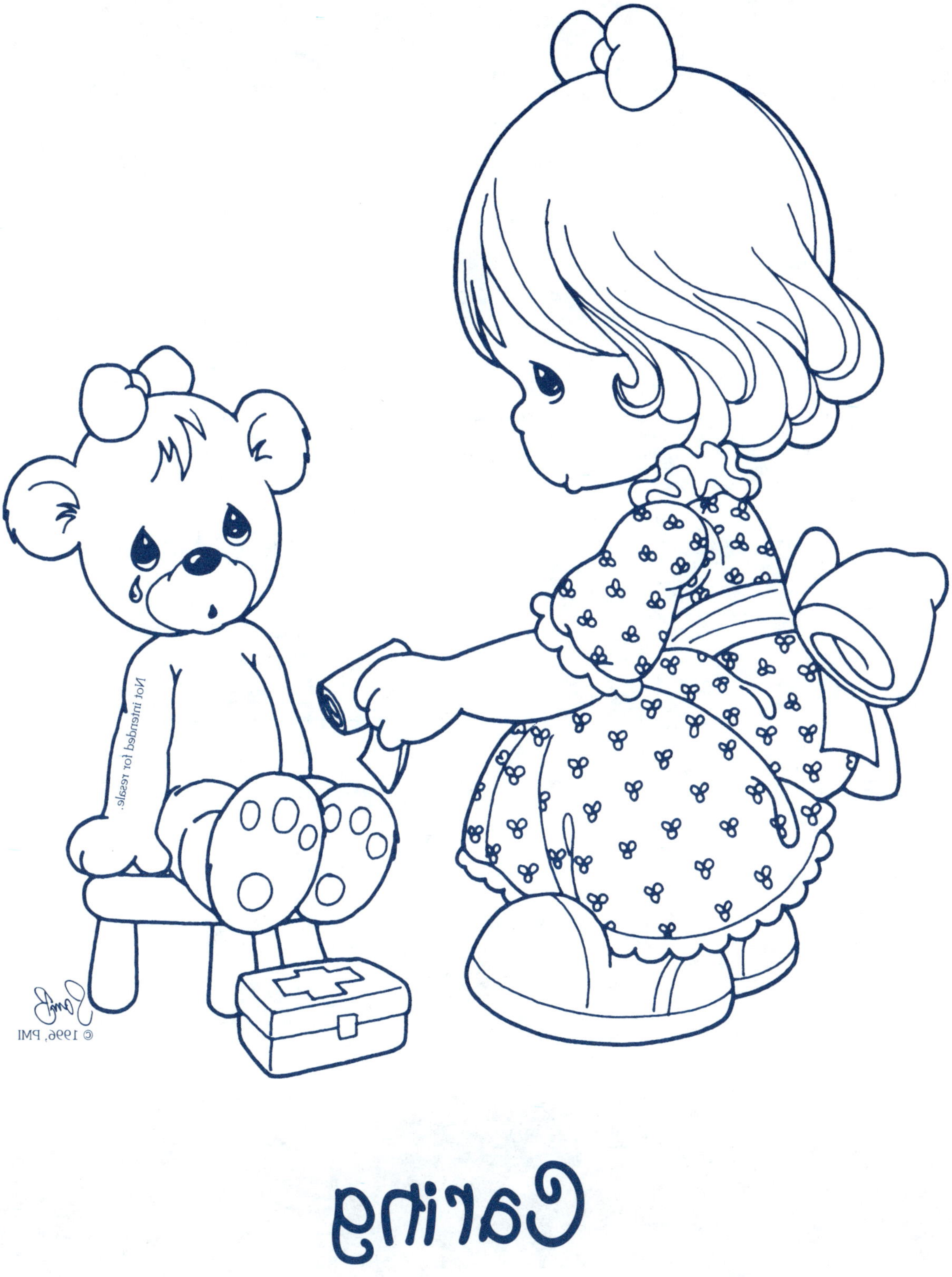

Caring

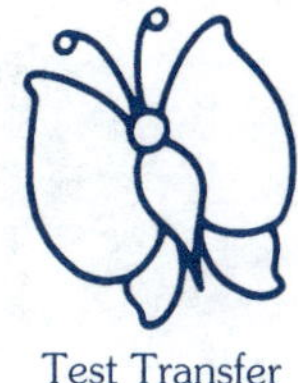

Test Transfer

Not intended for resale.
© 1996, PMI

Sharing

Sharing

Sharing

Test Transfer

Loving

Loving

Test Transfer

Not intended for resale.

© 1996, PMI

Caring

Caring

Test Transfer

Not intended for resale.
© 1996, PMI

Sharing

Sharing

Sharing

We Are God's Workmanship

We Are God's Workmanship

Test Transfer

We Are God's Workmanship

Not intended for resale.

© 1996, PMI

We Are God's Workmanship

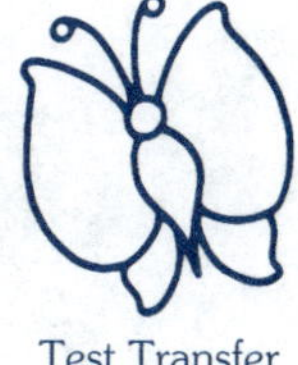

Test Transfer

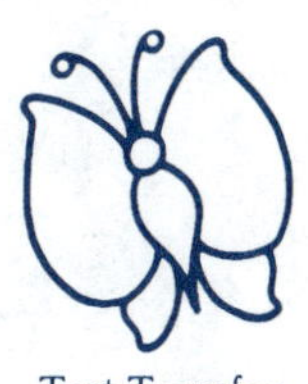

Test Transfer

Test Transfer

God's Promises Are Sure

God's Promises Are Sure

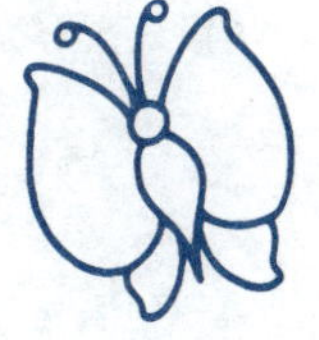

Test Transfer

I Believe In The Old Rugged Cross

I Believe In The Old Rugged Cross

Test Transfer

Not intended for resale.

© 1996, PMI

He Upholdeth Those Who Fall

He Upholdeth Those Who Fall

He Upholdeth Those Who Fall

Test Transfer

© 1996, PMI

Not intended for resale.

You Can Fly

You Can Fly

Test Transfer

Praise The Lord Anyhow

Not intended for resale.

© 1996, PMI

Praise The Lord Anyhow

Test Transfer

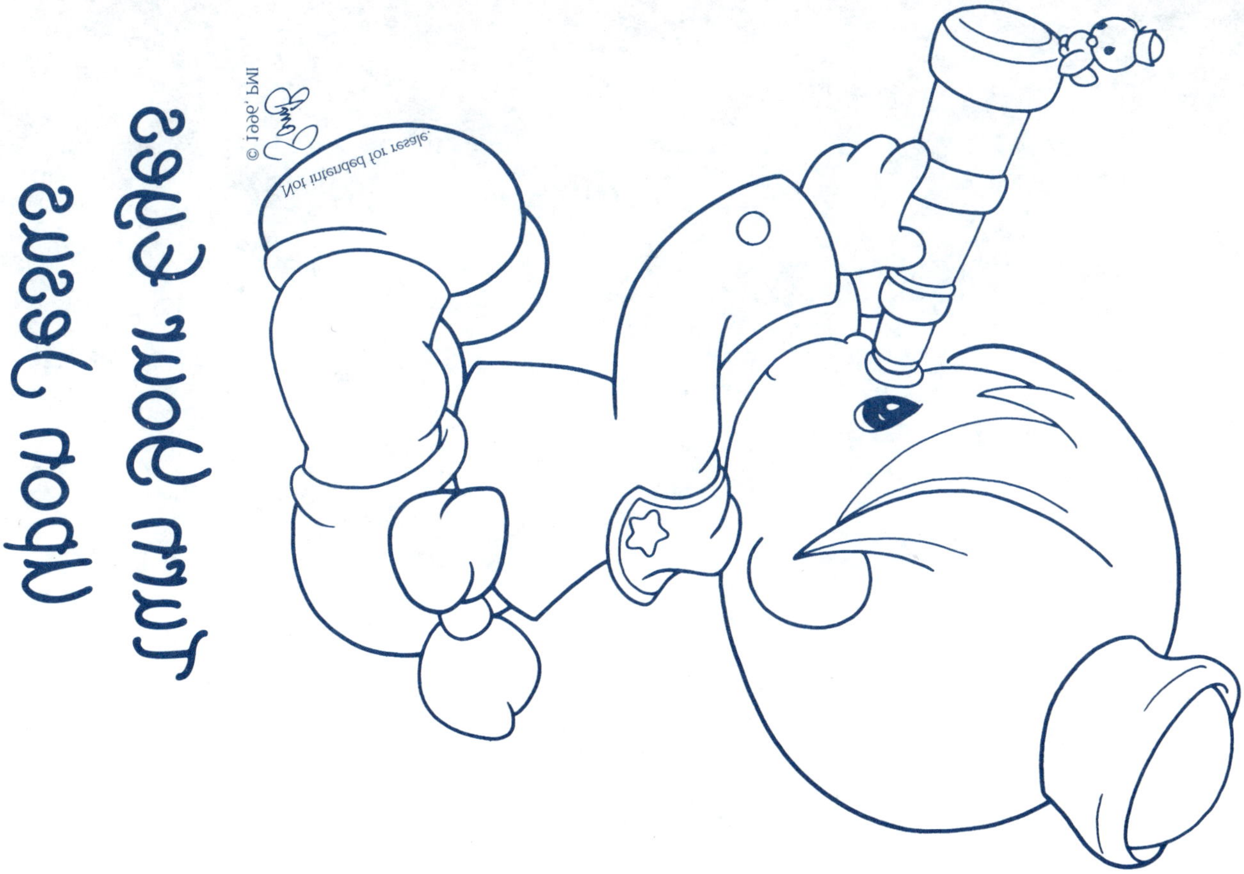

Turn Your Eyes Upon Jesus

I Believe In Miracles

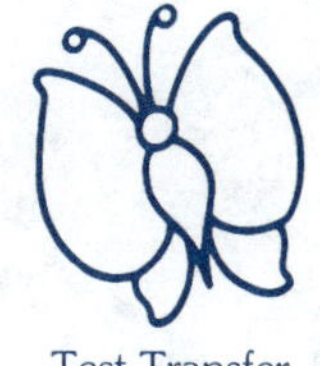

Test Transfer

Not intended for resale.
© 1996, PMI

It Is No Secret What God Can Do

It Is No Secret What God Can Do

It is No Secret
What God Can Do

Test Transfer

He Loves The Last, The Lost, And The Least

Test Transfer

Seeds

Not intended for resale.

© 1996, PMI

The Lord Will Provide

The Lord Will Provide

Test Transfer

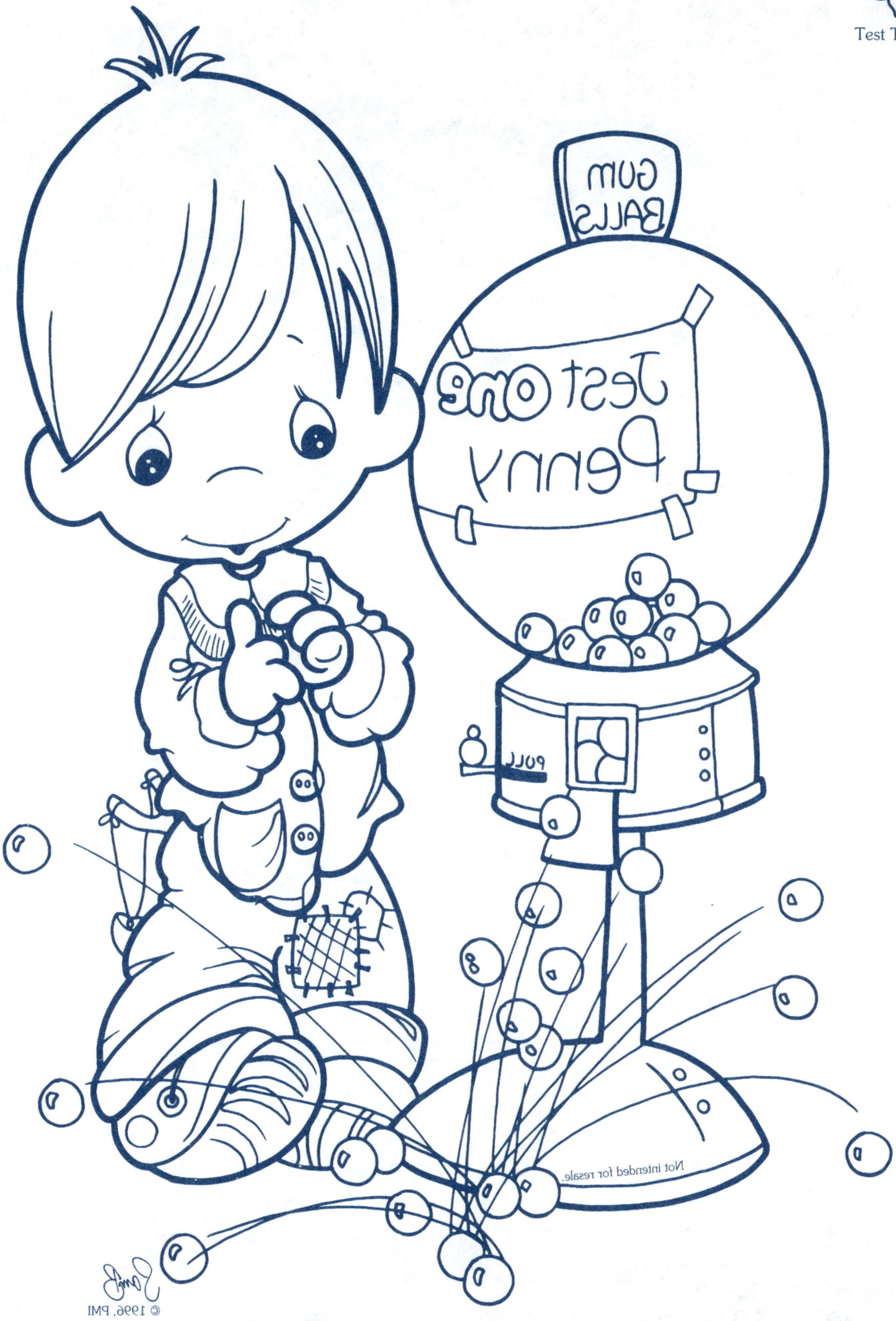

Not intended for resale.

© 1996, PMI

Test Transfer

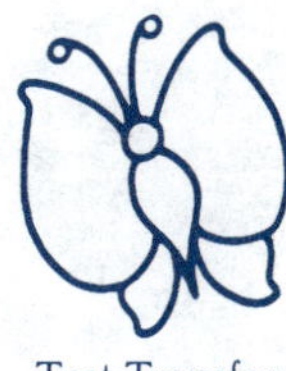

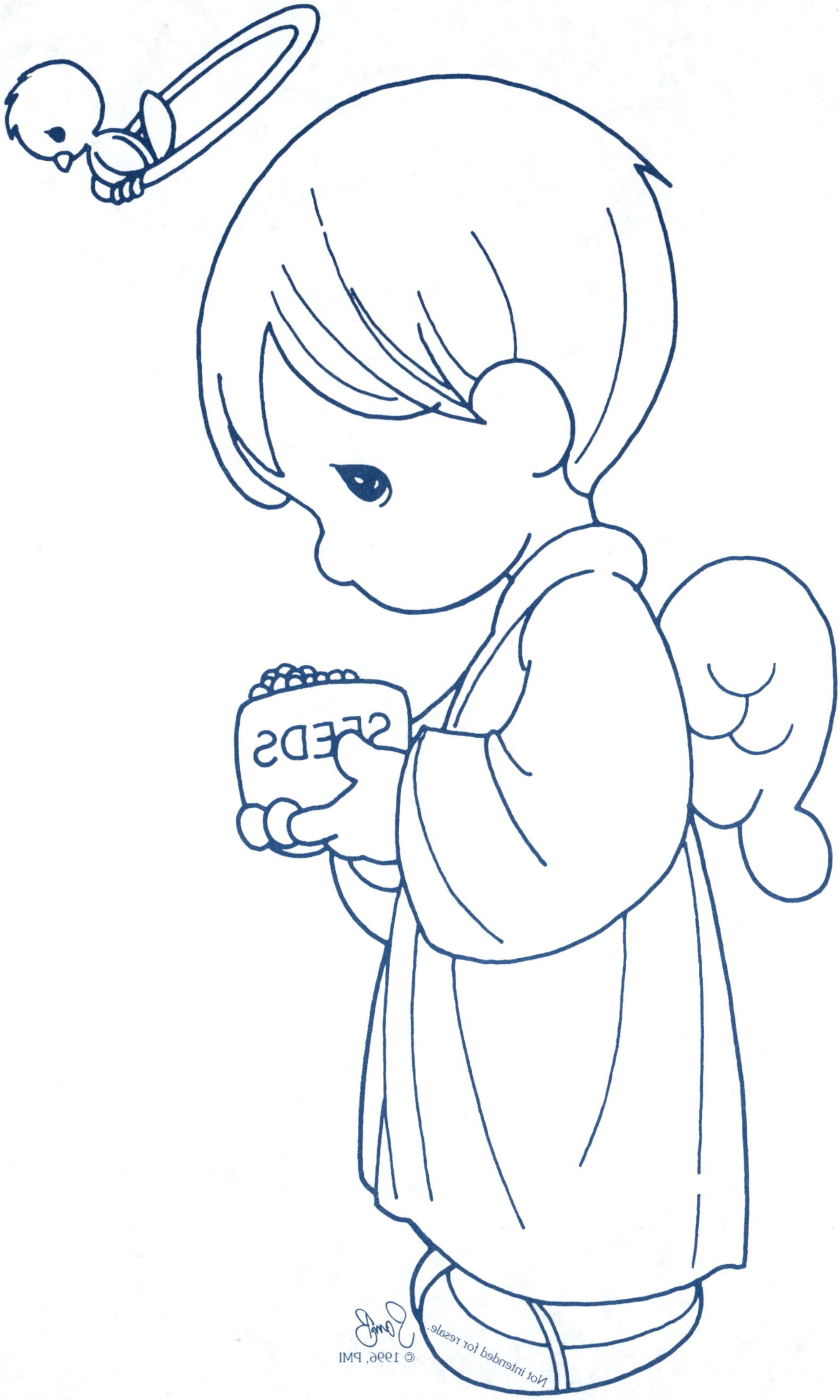
SEEDS
© 1996, PMI
Not intended for resale.

Test Transfer
Not intended for resale.
© 1996, PMI

Test Transfer

Test Transfer

Not intended for resale.

© 1996, PMI

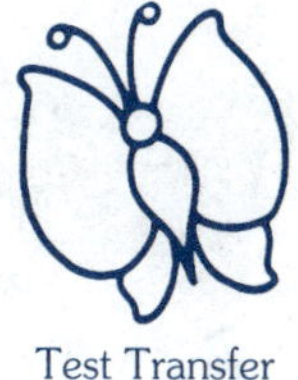

Test Transfer

Not intended for resale.
© 1996, PMI

God Loveth A Cheerful Giver

God Loveth A Cheerful Giver

Test Transfer

Not intended for resale.
© 1996, PMI

Test Transfer

Not intended for resale.

© 1996, PMI

An Event Worth Wading For

An Event Worth Wading For

Test Transfer

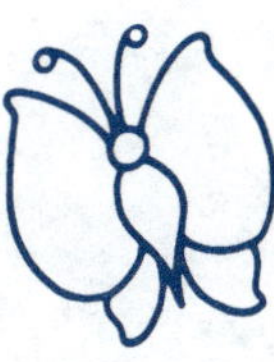

Test Transfer

CLICK

Not intended for resale.

© 1996, PMI

Test Transfer
© 1996, PMI
Not intended for resale.

Test Transfer

Not intended for resale.

© 1996, PMI

We All Have Our Bad Hair Days

We All Have Our Bad Hair Days

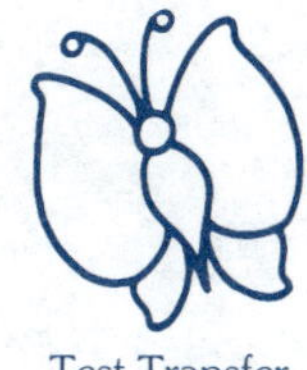

Test Transfer

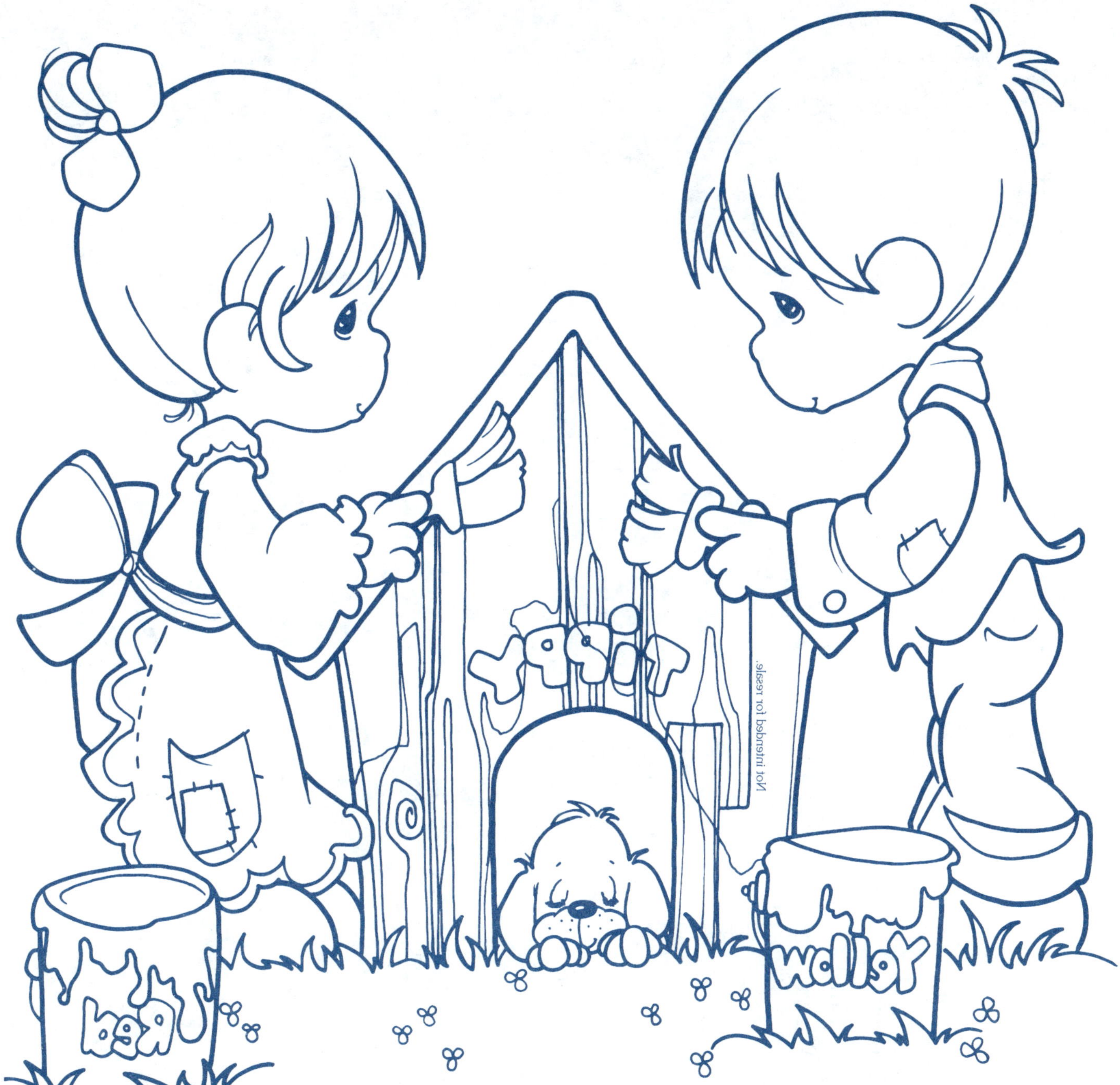

Tippy
Red
Yellow
Not intended for resale.

© 1996, PMI

Bless This House

Bless This House

Test Transfer

Not intended for resale.

© 1996, PMI

We Are All Precious In His Sight

We are All Precious In His Sight

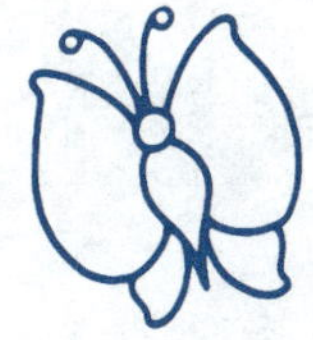

Test Transfer

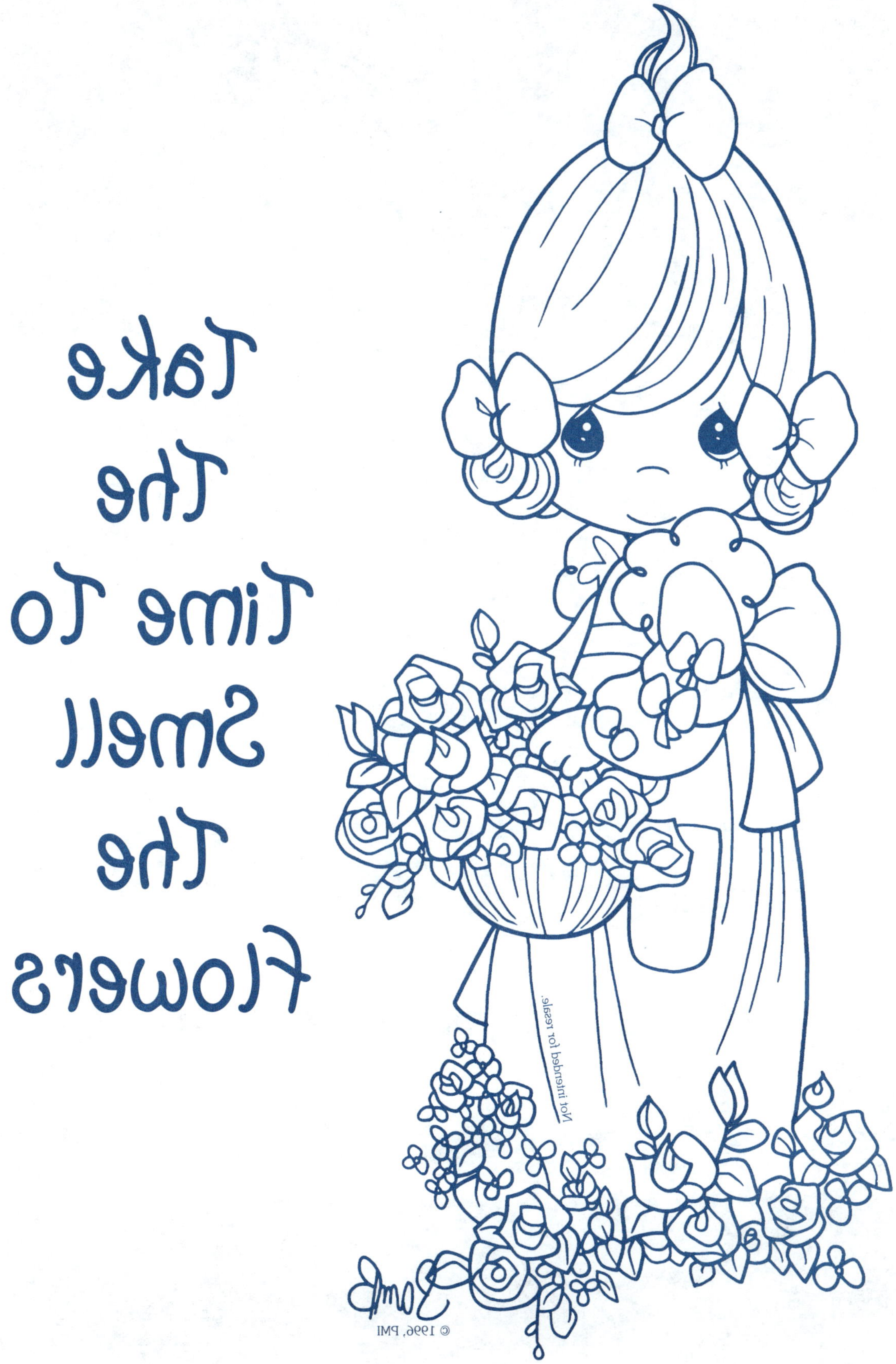
Take
The
Time To
Smell
The
Flowers
Not intended for resale.
© 1996, PMI

Take The Time To Smell The Flowers

Test Transfer

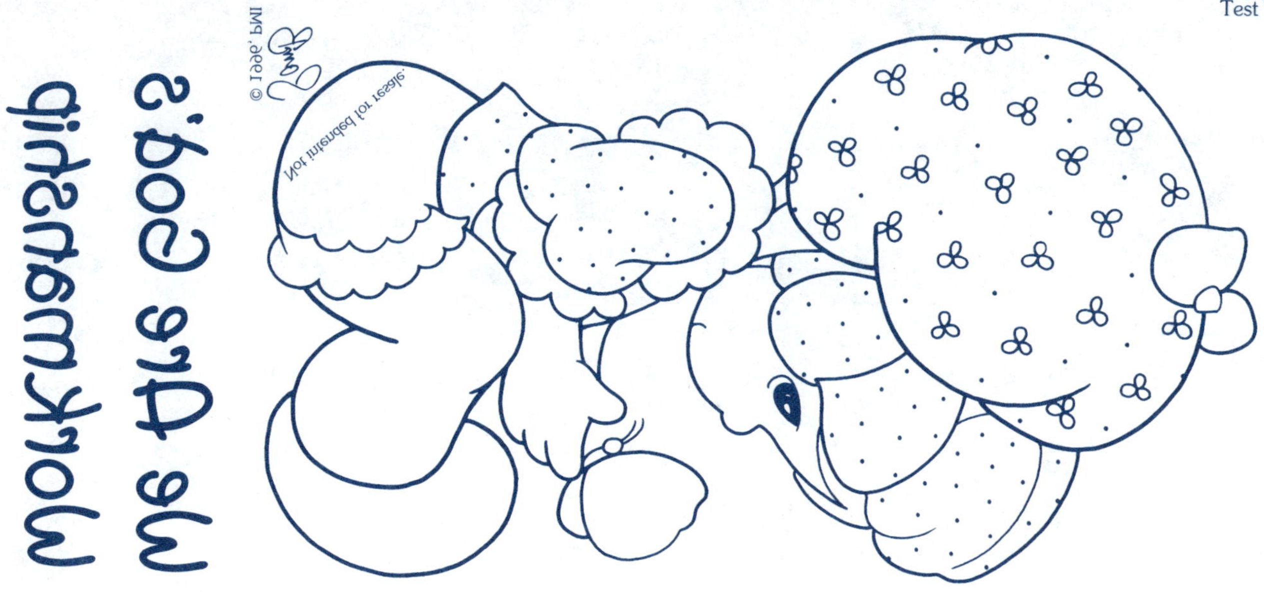

We Are God's Workmanship

You Have Touched So Many Hearts

He Cleansed My Soul

He Cleansed My Soul

Hallelujah For The Cross

Hallelujah For The Cross

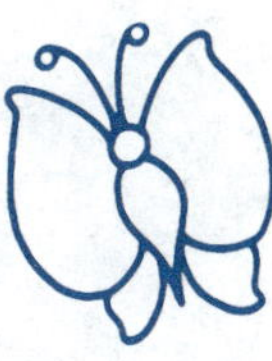

Test Transfer

Not intended for resale.

© 1996, PMI

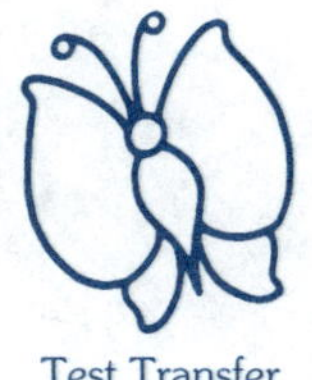

Test Transfer

Not intended for resale.

© 1996, PMI

Color Your World With Thanksgiving

Color Your World With Thanksgiving

Test Transfer

We Gather Together To Ask The Lord's Blessing

We Gather Together To Ask The Lord's Blessing

Test Transfer

Test Transfer

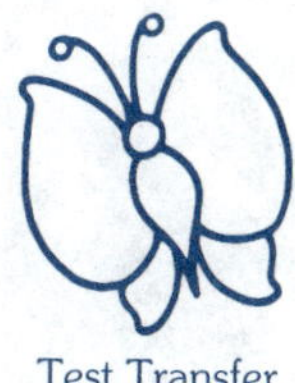

Test Transfer

Blessings To You

© 1996, PMI
Not intended for resale.

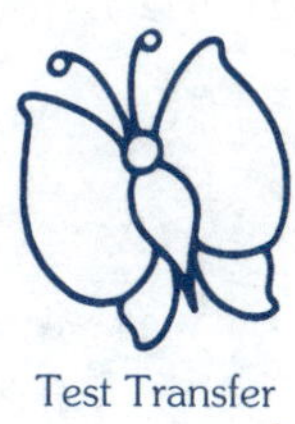

Test Transfer

Not intended for resale.
© 1996, PMI

Test Transfer

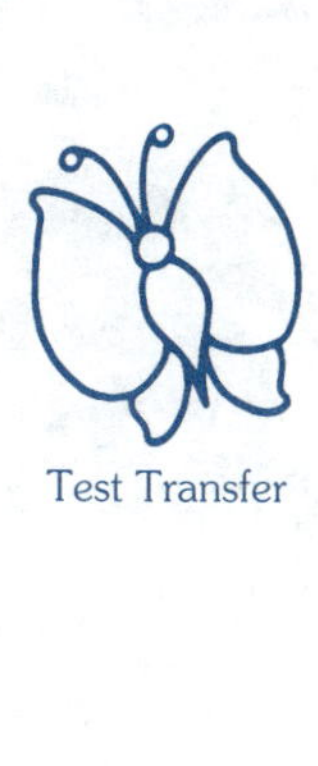

Test Transfer

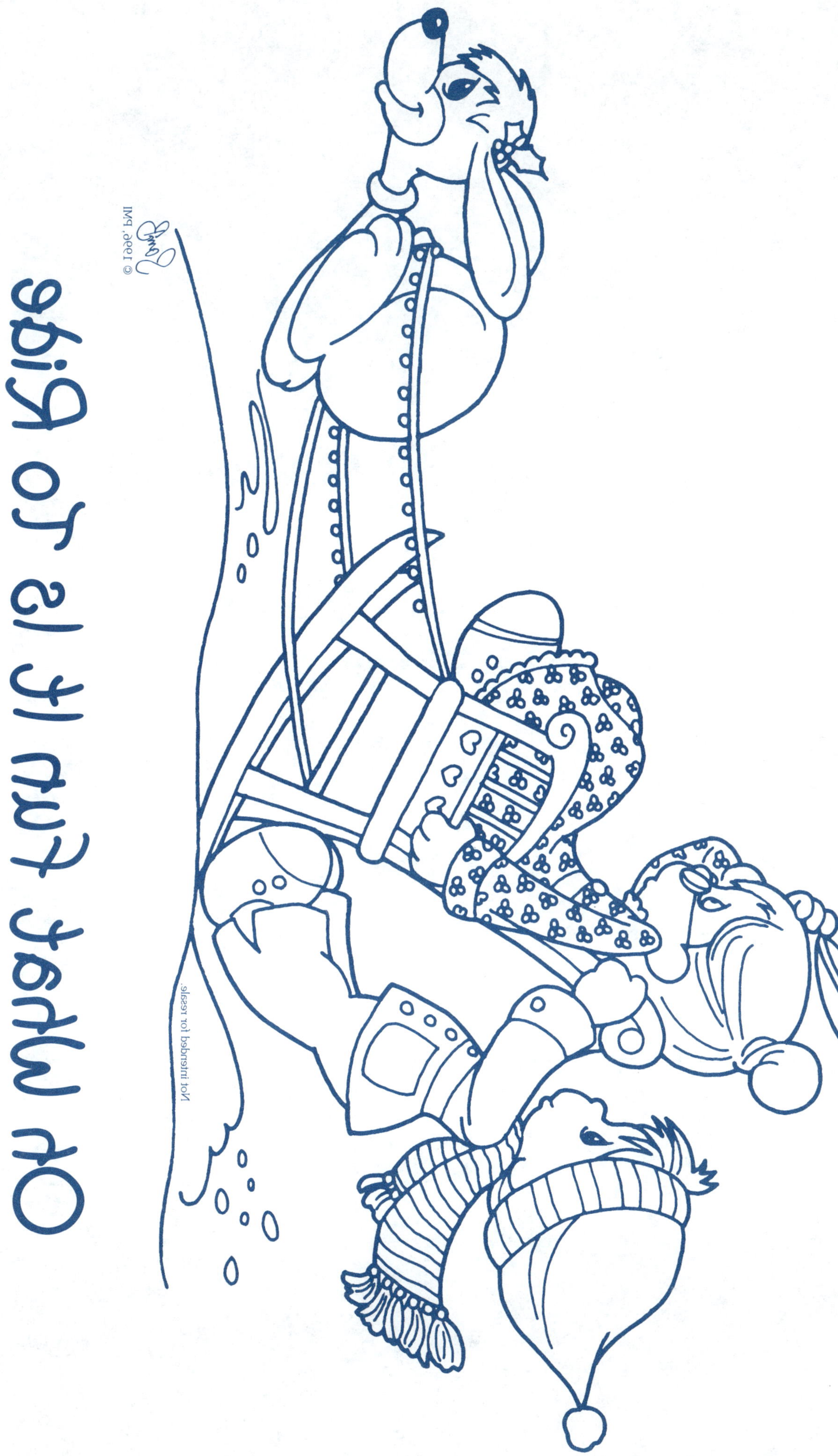

Oh What Fun It Is To Ride

© 1996, IMP

Not intended for resale

Oh What Fun It Is To Ride

Test Transfer

Not A Creature Was Stirring

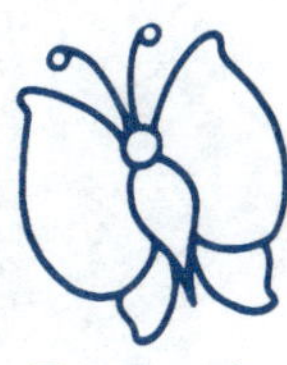

Test Transfer

Not intended for resale.

© 1996, PMI

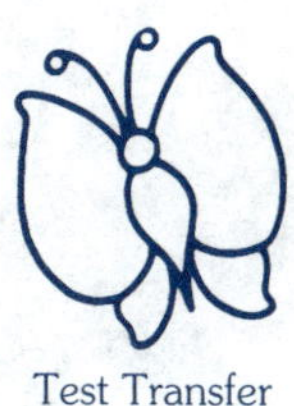

Test Transfer

Baby's First Christmas

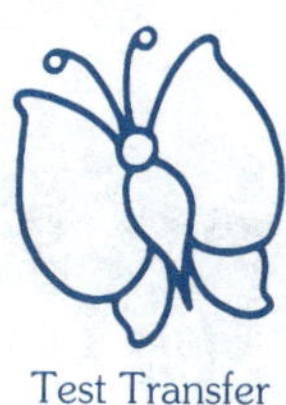

Test Transfer

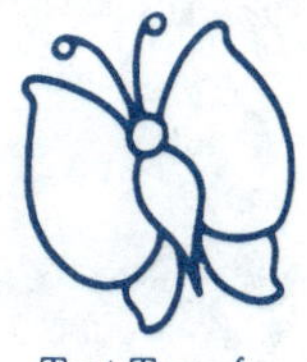

Test Transfer

Not intended for resale.

© 1996, PMI

Merry Christmoose

Merry Christmoose

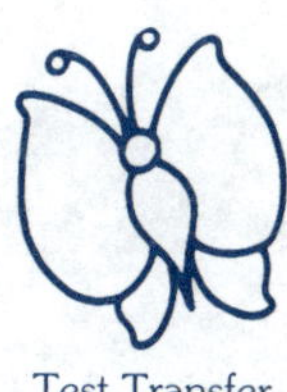

Test Transfer

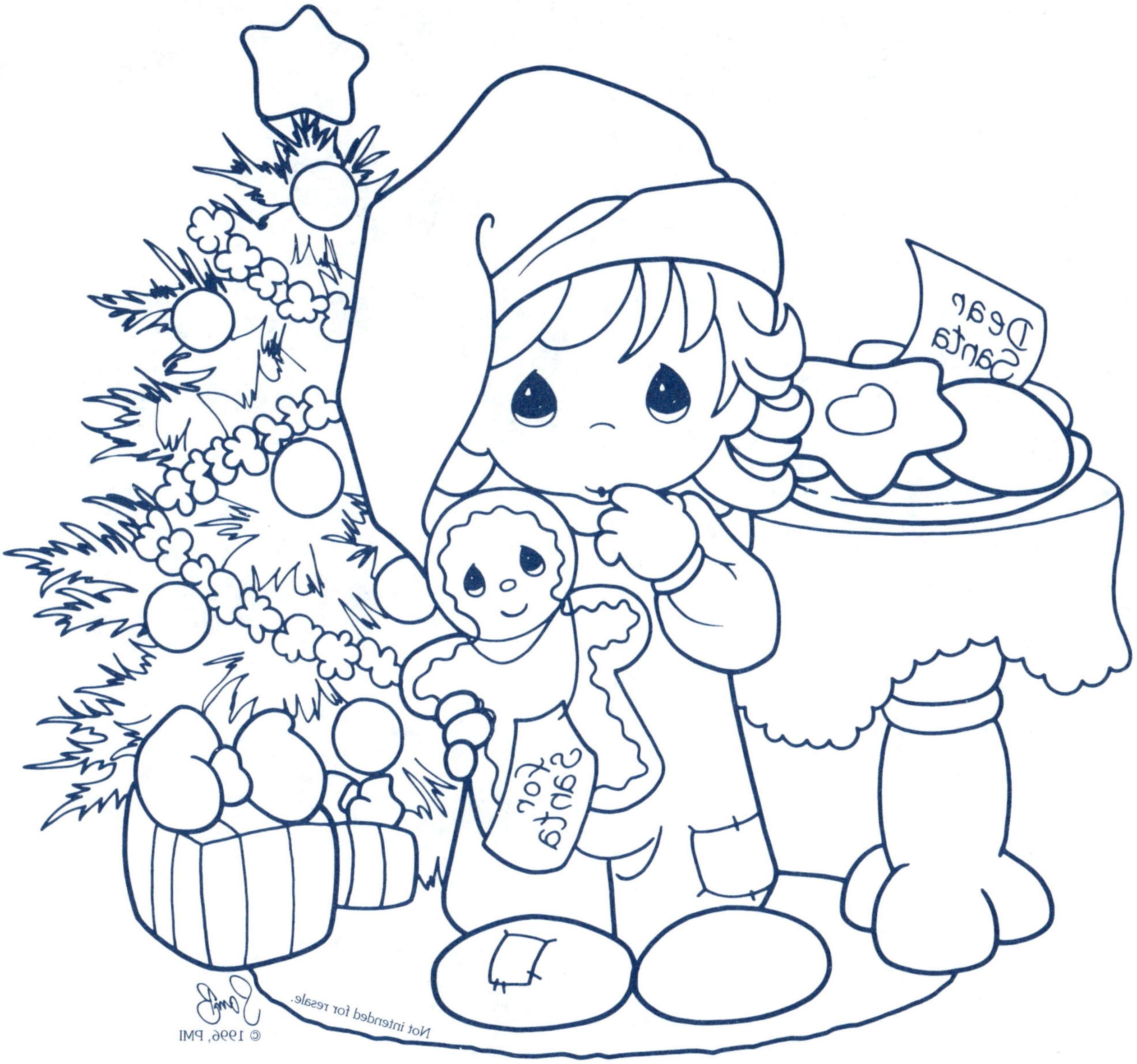

Not intended for resale.
© 1996, PMI

Test Transfer

The Greatest Gift Is A Friend

The Greatest Gift
A Friend

Test Transfer

May Your Christmas Be Warm

Wood Box

Not intended for resale.

© 1996, PMI

May Your Christmas Be Warm

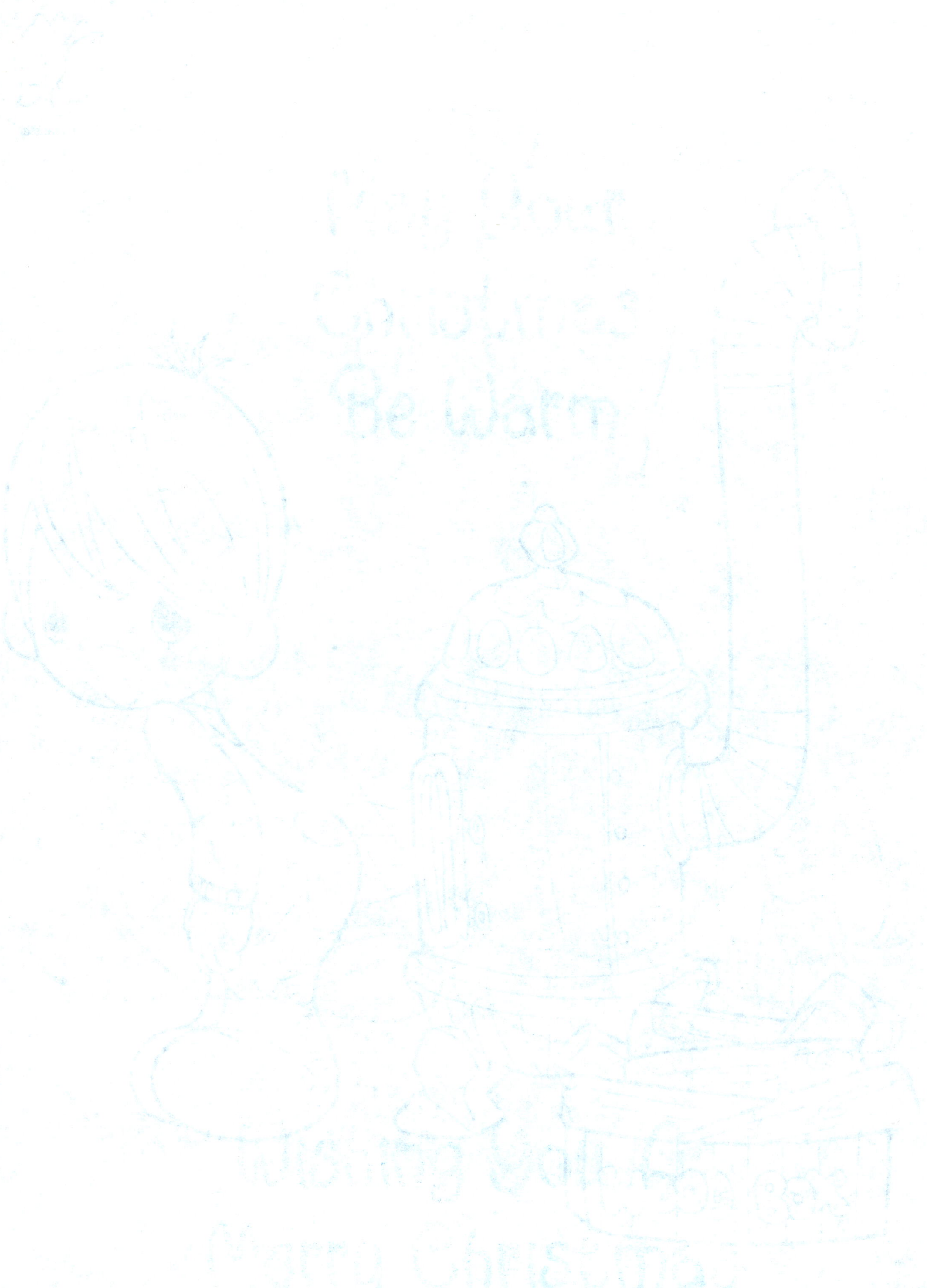

Be Warm

Merry Christmas

Wishing You A
Merry Christmas

Wishing You A Merry Christmas

Test Transfer
Silent Night
Not intended for resale.
© 1996, PMI

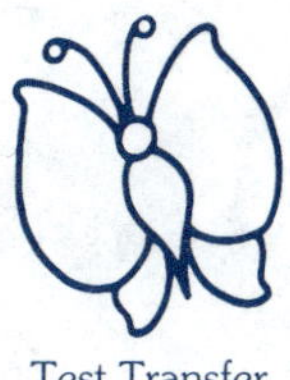

Test Transfer

Not intended for resale.

© 1996, PMI

Surrounded With Joy

Surrounded With Joy

Surrounded with Joy

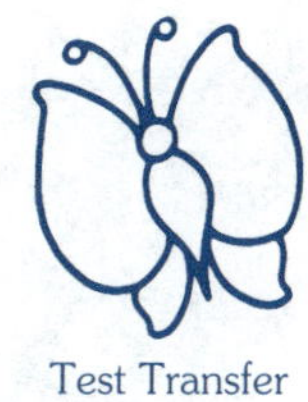

Test Transfer

May All Your Christmases
Be White

May All Your Christmases Be White

Test Transfer

Bundles Of Joy

Test Transfer

Test Transfer

They followed the star

Test Transfer

Not intended for resale.

© 1996, PMI

I'll Give Him My Heart

I'll Give Him My Heart

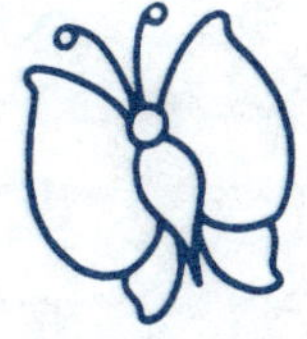

Test Transfer

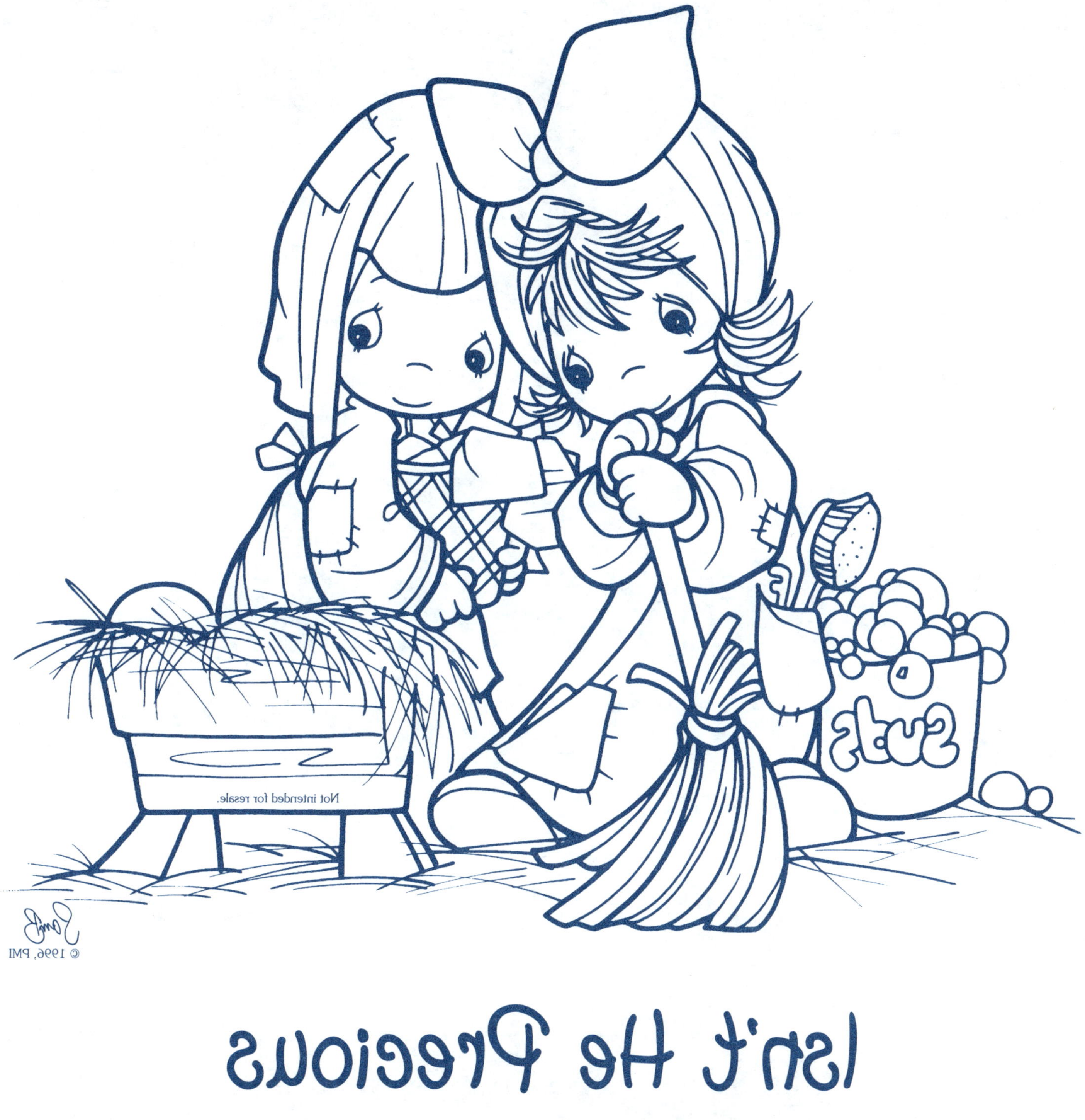

Suds
Not intended for resale.
© 1996, PMI
Isn't He Precious

Isn't He Precious

Test Transfer

Not intended for resale.

© 1996, PMI

Come Let Us Adore Him

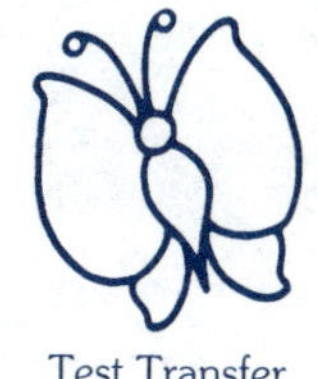

Test Transfer

Not intended for resale.

© 1996, PMI

O Come Let Us Adore Him

O Come Let Us Adore Him

O Come Let Us Adore Him

O Come Let Us Adore Him

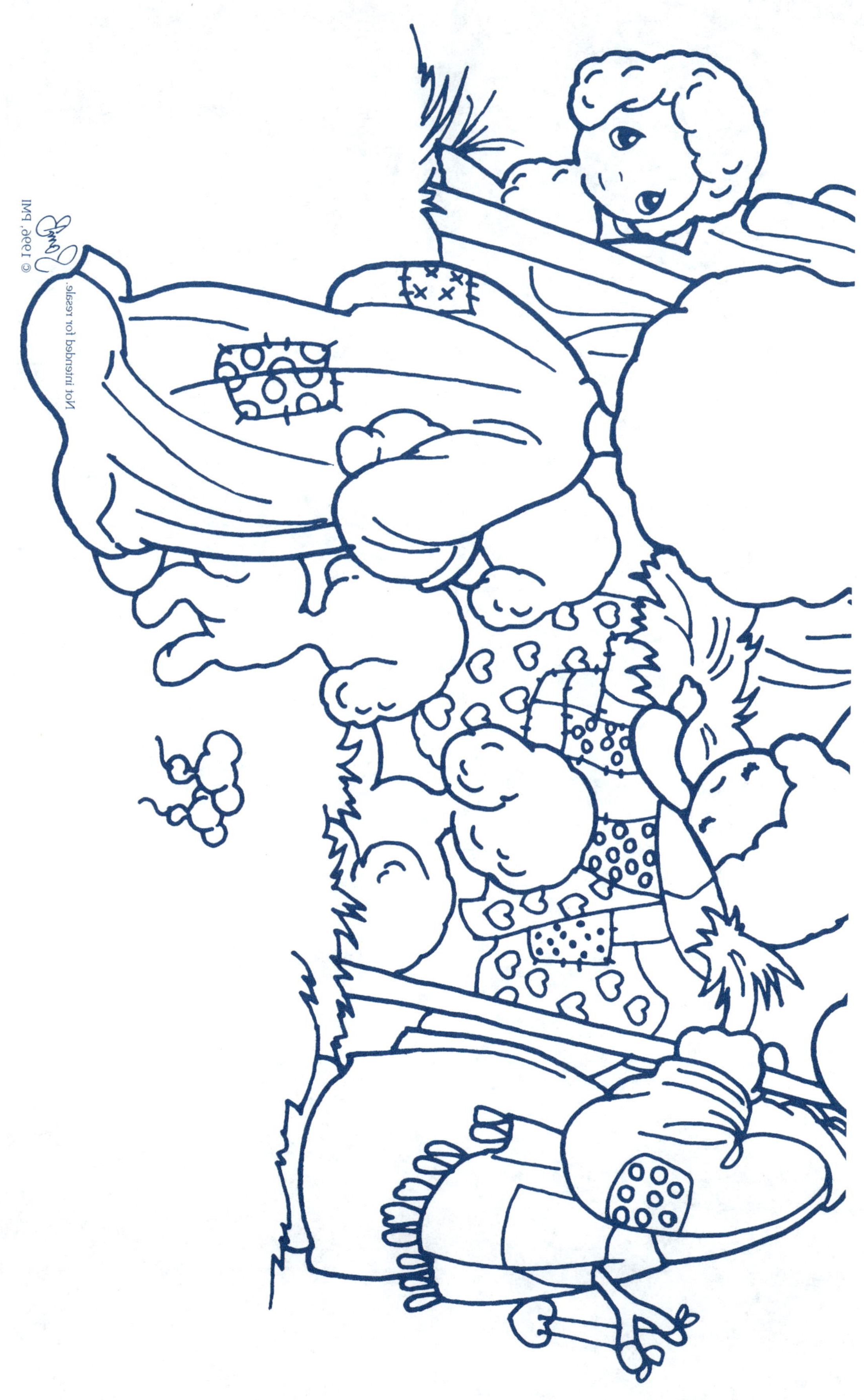

O Come Let Us Adore Him

Test Transfer

O Come Let Us Adore Him

Test Transfer

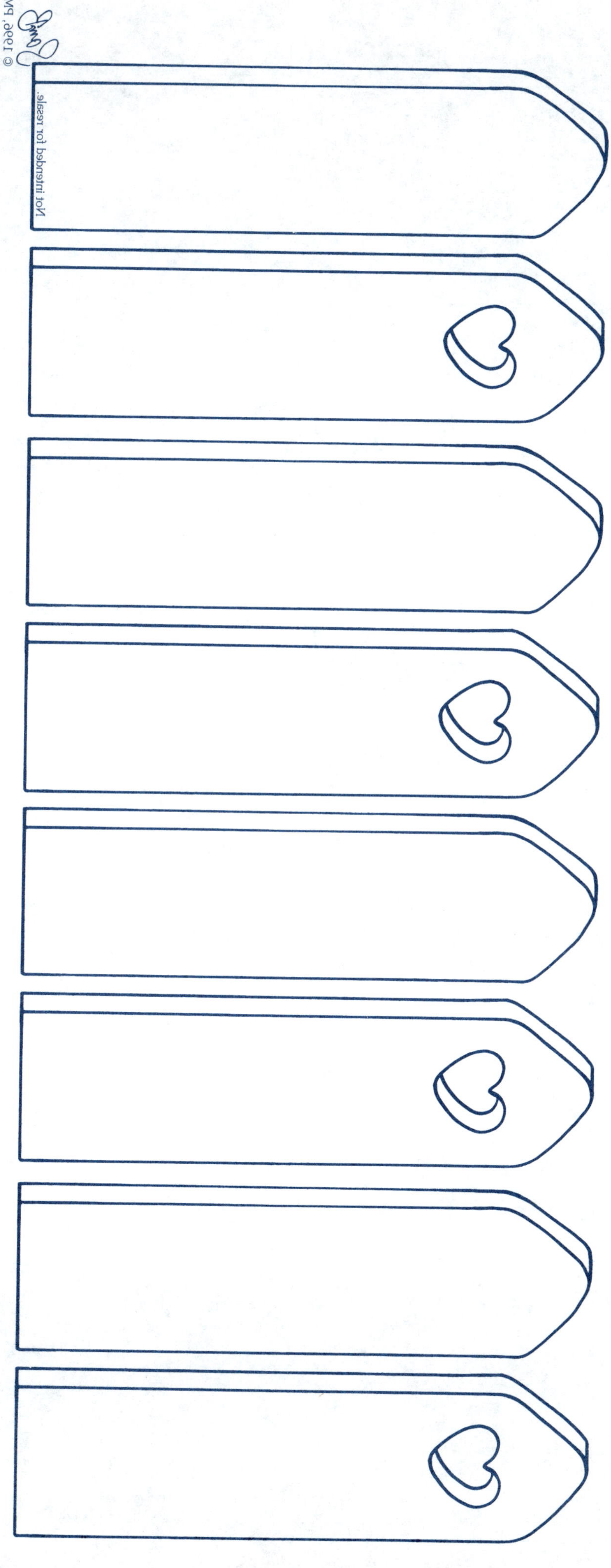

© 1996, PMI
Not intended for resale.

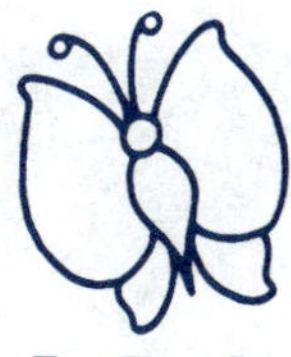
Test Transfer

© 1996, PMI
Not intended for resale.

© 1996, PMI
Not intended for resale.

Test Transfer
© 1996, PMI
Not intended for resale.

Test Transfer
© 1996, PMI
Not intended for resale.

Alphabets and Numbers — We've included several sizes of alphabets and numbers for you to personalize your projects. There is no right or wrong spacing between letters and words; arrange the letters in a manner pleasing to you. To play with the arrangement of letters and words, first cut out the letters you need. Arrange and rearrange letters as you like on your project, leaving a space for letters used more than once. When you have decided on placement, tape the letters together on the uninked side with Hot Tape. Place words, ink side down, on project and transfer.

© 1996, PMI
Not intended for resale.

0 1 2 3 4 5 6 7 8 9

a b c d e f g A B C D E F G

h i j k l m n H I J K L M N

o p q r s t u O P Q R S T

v w x y z U V W X Y Z

0 1 2 3 4 5 6 7 8 9

a b c d e f A B C D E F

g h i j k l m n G H I J K L M N

o p q r s t O P Q R S T

u v w x y z U V W X Y Z

Test Transfer

A B C D E F G H I J

K L M N O P Q R S

T U V W X Y Z

0 1 2 3 4 5 6 7 8 9

a b c d e f g h i j

k l m n o p q r s

t u v w x y z

0 1 2 3 4 5 6 7 8 9

© 1996, PMI
Not intended for resale.

A B C D E F G H I J

K L M N O P Q R S

T U V W X Y Z

0 1 2 3 4 5 6 7 8 9

a b c d e f g h i j

k l m n o p q r s

t u v w x y z

0 1 2 3 4 5 6 7 8 9